Routledge Revivals

Problems of a New World

First published in 1921, *Problems of a New World* deals with the economic and political issues that arose from the First World War. The first three parts of the study consider the world before the war, and the interests, purposes and ideals which influenced the national psyche during the years which followed. In the final two parts, Hobson assesses the political and economic conditions confronted by the post-war world, with a particular focus on the impact of war on industry, labour and the ideals of nationhood. This is an important work, of great interest to modern European and economic historians and students.

Problems of a New World

J. A. Hobson

Routledge
Taylor & Francis Group
LONDON AND NEW YORK

First published in 1921
by George Allen & Unwin Ltd

This edition first published in 2013 by Routledge
2 Park Square, Milton Park, Abingdon, Oxon, OX14 4RN

Simultaneously published in the USA and Canada
by Routledge
711 Third Avenue, New York, NY 10017

Routledge is an imprint of the Taylor & Francis Group, an informa business

Publisher's Note
The publisher has gone to great lengths to ensure the quality of this reprint but points out that some imperfections in the original copies may be apparent.

Disclaimer
The publisher has made every effort to trace copyright holders and welcomes correspondence from those they have been unable to contact.

A Library of Congress record exists under LC control no: 21008551

ISBN 13: 978-0-415-82077-6 (hbk)
ISBN 13: 978-0-203-55200-1 (ebk)

PROBLEMS OF A NEW WORLD

PROBLEMS OF A NEW WORLD

BY

J. A. HOBSON

LONDON: GEORGE ALLEN & UNWIN LTD
RUSKIN HOUSE, 40 MUSEUM STREET, W.C. 1

First published in 1921

PREFACE

PEOPLE are just beginning to understand that the break-up of the political system of Europe in 1914 was a bigger, a more complex and a more prolonged process than appeared when the split took place. We now know that the armed conflict during the four years that followed was but the first act in a drama destined to extend its *mise en scène* and to complicate its plot until the whole world became its stage and all its peoples actors.

New cracks continue to break up the old system into a variegated pattern of disorder, as the shock of the international struggle spreads to outlying areas and strikes into the internal structure of the several nations, making fresh fissures in their social-economic fabric. States and their constitutions, the ownership of property, the control of industry and the prevailing methods of distributing its product, every established institution, Church, Class, Party, down to the primordial unit, the Family, are subjected to new disruptive strains, and their affrighted guardians are fumbling after schemes of structural repair.

The reason why they fumble is that they have failed to take account of certain important revelations which the tumultuous events of these years have made regarding that Human Nature which is the operative principle in History. My object in these chapters is to focus these war lights so as to provide some clearer understanding of the practical problems that demand solution if a New World of order and progress is to emerge.

In the performance of this task three related issues present themselves for treatment. First, we must get a reliable revaluation of our pre-war world, in order to learn why and how we were deceived in our belief in its stability and strength. We next proceed to a close inspection of our national psychology and that of other nations, as disclosed in the glow and heat of war, with particular consideration of the ideals which inspired us and the fate which befell them after their fire died down.

In the light of this clearer understanding of our desires, interests and purposes we may then endeavour to formulate and assess those urgent tasks of political and economic reformation, or revolution, which the world to-day confronts or evades, and to take cognizance of certain new problems, racial, national, economic, which are gathering shape under the changed conditions which this New World presents.

The opening chapter of the book has been published in a recent issue of the *Political Science Quarterly Review*. Chapter II of Part IV, " The Liberation of Labour," was printed in the *Contemporary Review* of December 1920, and portions of Parts II and III, dealing with the " Civilian War-Mind " and the " Tragi-Comedy of Idealism " have appeared in the pages of *The Nation*. I am indebted to the editors of these publications for permission to republish these articles.

J. A. HOBSON.

HAMPSTEAD,
December 1920.

CONTENTS

CONTENTS

PART IV

THE NEW INDUSTRIAL REVOLUTION

PART V

A NEW WORLD

PART I

COLLAPSE OF THE OLD ORDER

CHAPTER I

THE SURPRISE OF 1914

WAR fell upon us late in the summer of 1914 as a terrible surprise. Hardly anybody had believed in its coming. A handful of dismal pacifists in the different countries pointing to the growth of armaments had uttered their vaticinations. Little knots of ardent militarists with their business companions, bent upon increased preparedness, talked confidently of the inevitable day, forgetting to reconcile this announcement with the preventive virtues they attributed to preparations. But few even of these extremists of the right and left seriously believed that war was imminent. There were, no doubt, a few in Germany and elsewhere who in the latter days believed in war because they had contrived it and determined it. But for our immediate purposes these may stand out of the account.

It is this general surprise and the ignorance to which it testifies that demand explanation. How came it about that people of every grade of knowledge and intelligence were so utterly blind as to the state of the world in the spring of 1914 ? The unthinking have chosen to compare the event with some catastrophe of nature or to dramatize it as a desperate crime of the rulers of a single nation. But though there is an element of truth in both of these explanations, neither affords reasonable satisfaction. For to make such a catastrophe or such a crime seem possible, the whole world and the people in it must have been hugely different from what we all thought them. Not different, however, in containing facts and forces that had lain hidden from our ken and were suddenly lit up for us by the red glare. Not one of the concrete issues which carried the seeds of strife, not one of the deep-seated divergencies of policy, not one of the fierce suspicions, hates, ambitions and cupidities in which danger might lurk but was exposed to innumerable watchful eyes. There was no lack of knowledge of the danger areas or of the dangers which they held. But in spite of all this knowledge the general sense of security was not seriously shaken. It was as in the days of Noah, but without the pretext the people then had for not listening to the idle *ipse dixit* of a senile croaker.

This false security was the product of a habitual misvaluation of the contentious forces and their counter-checks. The former were gravely underestimated, while heavily inflated value was given to the latter. Both errors are attributable to a single source, an excessive appreciation of men's moral and rational attainments and of the part they actually played in the guidance of individual and collective conduct. The doctrine of the perfectibility of man implicit in every higher religion, coupled with a faith in the power of enlightened self-interest to accomplish swift reforms in the fabric of human society, lay at the root of all the liberal revolutionary movements of the half-century that followed the French Revolution. The world was so constituted that everyone, in striving to preserve his own life and to promote his own happiness, was impelled along lines of conduct that conduced to the welfare of others. But he was also a social being in feeling and will, capable of conscious effort for the good of others and taking pleasure in every task of mutual aid. Sometimes the stress was laid upon enlightened selfishness, sometimes upon the social emotions. In either case, human relations were conceived as grounded in rationality, forming a system that was rational, appealing to the human reason for its operation.

The greatest moral discovery of the nineteenth century, that man belonged body and soul to the natural world, and that the whole of his life and conduct was subject to the reign of law, had profound reactions upon social thought and policy, especially in the spheres of statecraft and industry. Though the immediate philosophic fruit of this discovery was determinism, this rational creed had nothing in common with the paralysing fatalism charged against it by orthodox critics. On the contrary, it suffered at the hands of its chief exponents from an excessive faith in the power of man to mould his destiny, adapting and creating institutions for his wholesome needs and desires with an ease and a celerity that made light of the human heritage of habits and attachments. It is impossible to follow the various currents of reforming zeal from Godwin, Shelley and the youthful Coleridge through the more definite proposals and experiments of Bentham, Owen, J. S. Mill and their philosophical-radical, Chartist and socialist followers, without confronting a belief in man's power to be the arbiter of his fate quite staggering in the measure of its confidence. Bentham's contempt for history was indeed characteristic of his liberalism, which demanded as complete as possible a liberation from all trammels of the past. Though commonly coupled with repudiation of existing religious dogmas, this nineteenth-century rationalism conducted itself with the fervour of religious zeal.

The faith in reason rested upon two assumptions. First, that reason was by right, and in fact, the supreme arbiter in human conduct; and second, that a complete harmony of human relations was discoverable and attainable by getting reason to prevail in individual and national affairs. "Getting reason to prevail" meant opening wide the portals to knowledge and removing the positive barriers of law, tradition, prejudice and passion which blocked the play of enlightened self-interest. This faith, penetrating alike the individualism of Bentham and the socialism of Owen, may be regarded as a practical mysticism, deriving its nourishment partly from the philosophy of the Revolution, partly from the miraculous technology of the new machine industry. If applied reason can so immensely and so rapidly enlarge the bounds of material productivity, cannot the same power beneficially transform the entire structure of human society? Abundant wealth, equitably distributed by the operation of inevitable laws among the producers, would form the material basis of a new moral world. A free instructed people would co-operate in a hundred ways for their mutual advantage. Though one of these ways would be the State, political democracy was not a chief concern. For in the rational world the coercive arm of society would have little scope. The functions of the State were to be purely defensive, directed to prevent the interference of one person with another, within the national limits, and of one nation with another in the wider world of States and governments. The reasonable will of individual citizens would preserve harmony and promote social progress within the several nations and in the wider sphere of humanity, if only free play were secured for it. The State was conceived as an essentially artificial and repressive instrument, whose operation should be kept at a minimum. Hence it came about that the early socialistic proposals commonly gave the State the go-by and based themselves upon the purely voluntary association of individual citizens. This limited conception of the State imparted a certain unsubstantiality to the radical and chartist agitations for an extended franchise and other instruments of political democracy. These agitations were rather the indices of popular discontents, rooted in the miserable social-economic conditions of the working classes, than a firm and natural expression of the popular will seeking incorporation in the State. That is why they were dissipated in the mid-century by small political concessions floated on the rising tide of a trade prosperity which gave relief and hope to the organizing artisan classes that represented the lowest strata of political consciousness.

There was in the mid-century no clear recognition anywhere, save in a few eccentric or disordered brains, of the necessity and feasibility of converting and enlarging the machinery of government into a means of so controlling industry and distributing its fruits as to secure a reasonable livelihood for all and to remedy the palpable injustices in the apportionment of this world's goods. There had been plenty of shrewd and trenchant exposures of the abuses of land-ownership and of the factory system, with their related evils of unemployment, sweating wages, oppression of child-life, insanitary housing, poor-law degradation and the like. But though the State was looked to for supplying certain minor safeguards, the liberative tide was still in the ascendant, and the free play of enlightened self-interest in competitive industry was still the animating faith of the friends of popular progress.

This typical middle-class sentimental rationalism long succeeded in diverting popular self-government from all thoughts or plans of economic democracy. Though Mazzini as early as the late thirties had made his brilliant exposure of the futility of a political revolution which left the keys of industrial masterhood in the hands of a new capitalistic oligarchy, neither the mind nor the circumstances of any great people were ripe for its reception. The nationalistic spirit, guided by bourgeois leaders and ambitions, was a dominant factor in the continental revolutions of the mid-century, and the economic communism which flared up for a brief period in the large French cities was in reality little more than an ill-prepared by-product of a co-operative spirit which found more immediately profitable expression in trade-union and other non-political spheres of activity. The early socialism, alike of Owen and of the Christian socialists of the next generation, must properly rank as a variant of this bourgeois rationalism, inspired with a larger measure of social compunction and with a more conscious reliance upon the forces of human comradeship. The deep sentimentalism with which men like Kingsley and Maurice steeped their teaching should not hide this essential truth.

So long as the firm faith in a natural harmony of interests, personal and national, operating either through competition or the private co-operation of individuals, continued to be the prevailing creed of social reformers, there was little hope of effective organic reform. For neither the harder rationalism of the Manchester School nor the softer of the early socialism was capable of yielding a nutritious and stimulating gospel to the people. Its essential defects were two. The first was this open and persistent cleavage between political and industrial advancement, serving to enfeeble the democratic movement by removing from its scope the most vital and appealing issues. The second was the naïvely middle-class character of the politics and economics. In national and still more in local politics the new well-to-do business classes with their professional retinue were obtrusively dominant in all issues which either touched their pockets or their class pride. This dominance was not seriously impaired by the several extensions of the franchise succeeding the Reform Act of 1832 that first put them in the saddle. Their superior wealth, control over employment, dominant personality, prestige and organizing power, kept in their hands the levers of politics and enabled them with no great difficulty to influence and manipulate the widening working-class electorate. They continued to use this power so as to encourage the belief that substantial equality of opportunity existed and that personal character was everywhere an assured road to success and prosperity, while they prolonged the career of liberalism by concentrating the party struggle on numerous separate little liberative missions, conducted slowly and piecemeal, thus staving off the bigger organic reforms that were emerging in the new radicalism of the later half-century.

It was not a conscious statecraft, but the instinctive self-defence of the bourgeois politician. A free scope for private competitive enterprise alike in domestic industry and foreign trade, with such personal liberties and opportunities of education, movement, choice of trade, thrift and comfort for the workers, as would keep them industrious and contented with their lot and with the economic and political leadership of the employing middle classes—such was the prevailing thought of the men who boasted themselves the backbone of the country. It was not necessary or desirable to make it into a theory or a system. For that process was rather a hindrance than an aid to practice. Though able exponents of the theory presented themselves, the ruling bourgeoisie only assimilated fragments of the teaching. From their authoritative economists they took a few convenient dogmas, such as the law of rent and the wage fund, for weapons in their encounters with land-owners, trade-unions and meddling philanthropists. Their political philosophers and lawyers furnished a little rhetoric about freedom of contract, personal rights and the limits of legislative and administrative government, with which they eked out a confined but serviceable policy for their dealings with the State. The larger complexity of the philosophic radicalism never entered the brains or hearts of these hard, practical men, who knew what they wanted and meant to get it. Even the simpler gospel of Cobden, with its glow of moral fervour, had too much theory in it to prove acceptable to more than a little handful. His lamentations over the desertion of his principles of cosmopolitanism by the majority of those who heard him gladly, when he led them to cheap food and prosperous export trade, are an instructive testimony to the disinclination of the new dominant class for any coherent social thinking. The fate of the socialistic doctrines that later in the century displaced the mid-Victorian individualism was very similar. Neither the proletarian brand which German revolutionists had manufactured from the materials exported from this country and re-exported a generation later, nor the superior academic brand compounded of Rousseau, Hegel and T. H. Green, which, mixed with Jevonian economics, nourished the young lions of Fabianism, found any wide or deep acceptance among any class of our people. This, of course, does not imply that they were negligible as impelling or directive forces in the political and economic movements of the age. For though the ideologists vastly overrate the general influence of their ideas and isms in moulding human affairs, the cumulative value of the particular thoughts and sentiments and even formulas which they suggest to politicians, business men and practical reformers has been considerable, even in England, the country least susceptible to the direct and conscious guidance of ideas. What practical men take from theorists in Britain is pointers along roads that circumstances have already opened up for possible advance. Just as the theorizing of Adam Smith and Ricardo, working through the agitation of the anti-corn law leaguers, drove Peel and his politicians into a piecemeal free trade, so the new thinking on the positive functions of government led the municipal reformers of the eighties and nineties to tackle with more confidence their gas-and-water socialism and still later helped to remove some obstinate barriers to the development of national services for health, education and insurance.

Although there is a natural tendency just now to overstress every antithesis between our ways and those of Germany, it cannot be denied that a wide difference has existed in the operative force of theories and systems in the two countries. The disposition and the habit of working from thought-out purposes through plans into concrete arrangements is justly cited as the peculiar quality of Prussian social craft, from the time at least of Stein and Humboldt onward. Nor is it by any means confined to high politics. The contrast with our ways is even more striking in the subsidiary realms of education, transport, credit, town planning, insurance and industrial structure. Compare the development of our so-called railway system, our banking, the unlicensed spread of our great cities or the emergence of our business combines with those of Germany. Our way has been that of groping empiricism, not merely not believing in theories and preconcerted plans, but even disbelieving in them. There may at first sight seem to be an inconsistency between this view of our national way of going on and the rationalistic error which we found at the root of our failure to understand the state of the world in 1914. The contradiction, however, is only apparent, for at the root of our refusal to think out things in advance, to arrange consciously the forces adequate to attain a clearly conceived end, is a sort of half belief and half feeling that it doesn't pay to think out things. Our practice of tackling difficulties when they come, improvising ways of overcoming them, and in general of muddling through, we really hold to be a sound policy. Nor is this judgment or sentiment sheer mental inertia, or mere inability to think straight or far. It drives down to that rationalism which I have identified with practical mysticism in a conviction of the existence of some order in human affairs along the tide of which we may reasonably allow ourselves to float with confidence that somehow we shall reach the haven where we would be. We are opportunists on principle. That principle implies a generally favourable drift or tendency, or even providence, upon which we may rely to see us through and which dispenses with the obligation to practise much forethought. In America this is called the doctrine of manifest destiny. But we feel that even to make a conscious doctrine of it interferes with its spontaneity. The great historical example of this way of life is our Empire, rightly described as built up in a " fit of absence of mind." To Teutonic statecraft such a statement ranks as sheer hypocrisy, but none the less it is the truth. Individual builders there have been, and bits of personal planning, but never has the edifice of empire presented itself as an object of policy or even of desire to our government or people. Its general purpose can only be found in terms of drift or tendency. It will no doubt be urged that irrationalism is a more appropriate term than rationalism to describe this state of mind. But my point is that the state of mind implies a belief in the existence of some immanent reason in history working towards harmony and justifying optimism. Reason in the nature of things happily dispenses with the painful toil of clear individual thinking.

These general reflections may help to explain the universal surprise at the collapse of our world in 1914. For whether we regard the theorizing few or the many content with practice, we find no perception of the formidable nature of the antagonisms which for several generations had been gathering strength for open conflict. Even the historical commentators of to-day, as they survey and group into general movements the large happenings of the nineteenth century, often exhibit the same blindness which I have imputed to the current theorists. The smooth bourgeois optimism which characterized the liberal thinkers of the mid-century in their championship of nationalism, parliamentary institutions, broad franchise, free trade, capitalistic industry and internationalism, is discernible in the present-day interpreters of these movements. Take, for example, that widest stream of political events in Europe designated as the movement for national self-government. Historians distinguish its two currents or impulses, one making for national unity or government, the nation State in its completeness, and another seeking to establish democratic rule within the State. Correct in regarding this common flow and tendency of events as of profound significance, they have usually overvalued the achievements. On the one hand they have taken too formal a view of the liberative processes with which they deal, and on the other they have failed to appreciate the flaws in the working of the so-called democratic institutions.

The reign of machinery, the outward and visible sign of nineteenth-century progress, has annexed our very minds and processes of thinking. Mechanical metaphors have secretly imposed themselves upon our politics and squeezed out the humanity. That willing communion of intelligences which should constitute a party has become in name and in substance a "machine," politics are "engineered," and divergent interests are reconciled by "balances of power." I should be far from describing the great nationalist movement of the nineteenth century as mechanical. It was the product of passionate enthusiasms as well as of the play of reasonable interests. The struggle for liberation on the part of subject nationalities and for the gains of unification in the place of division broke out in a dozen different quarters during the first half of the century, and the two following decades saw the movement not indeed completed, but brought to a long halt in which splendid successes were recorded. In some cases, as in Germany and to a less extent in Italy, dynastic, military, fiscal and transport considerations were powerful propellers towards unification. But everywhere a genuinely national sentiment, based on a varying blend of racial, religious, linguistic and territorial community, gave force and nourishment to the new national structure. Its liberative and self-realizing virtues were garnered not in Europe alone. The foundations of the nationhood of our great overseas dominions were laid in the colonial policy of this epoch, while the breaking away of the Spanish-American colonies from their European attachment gave a great expansion of national self-government in the New World. But nationalism, regarded as the spirit and the practice of racial and territorial autonomy, has borne an exceedingly precarious relation to democracy. It has been consistent with the tyrannous domination of a dynasty, a caste or class, within the area of the nation. Indeed, at all times the spirit of nationality has been subject to exploitation by a dominant class for the suppression of internal discontents and the defence of privileges. Stein, Hardenberg, Bismarck and Treitschke used the enthusiasm of nationalism to fasten the fetters of a dominant Prussian caste upon the Germanic peoples. The struggles for the maintenance or the recovery of Polish and Hungarian national independence were directed by the ruling ambitions of an oppressive racial and economic oligarchy.

Professor Ramsay Muir, in his interesting study of the relations between nationality and self-government in the nineteenth century, greatly over-strains the actual association of the movements. If self-government signifies, as it should, the direct participation of the whole people in its government, though some temporary coincidence appears, there is as much antagonism as sympathy in the actual operation of the tendencies in modern history. Nationalism is used as often to avert as to feed democracy. For although the appeal to the racial unity and common spirit of a people for the assertion of its integrity and independence must indisputably tend to arouse in the common people a dignity and a desire to have a voice in public affairs, the leadership and prestige of military or political champions in the struggle may often suffice to foster or extort a servile consent of the governed as a feeble substitute for democracy. Indeed, it is precisely on this negative attribute that Professor Muir relies when he insists that " the land-owning aristocracy of the eighteenth century ruled Britain by consent " and that in Britain, France and Belgium after 1830 the " effective popular control of a government was henceforth solidly established.'

But the failure of a subject people or a subject class to revolt against its rulers is no true consent. Nor does the irregular connection between nationality and parliamentary government go far toward identifying nationalism with democracy as the typical achievement in the politics of the nineteenth century. None of the extensions of the franchise in Britain in 1832, 1867 and 1884 secured full and effective self-government for the people, or even for the enlarged electorate regarded as representative of the people. Historians and politicians alike have deceived themselves and others by a grave over-valuation of mere electoral machinery. Neither by the popularization of the franchise nor by the less formal operation of public opinion has the reality of democratic government been secured. The power of the aristo-plutocracy, somewhat changed in composition and demanding more cunning and discretion for its successful operation, still stands substantially unimpaired in Britain, France and America. The governing few still pump down their will through the organs of public opinion upon the electorate, to draw it up again with the formal endorsement of an unreal general will or consent of the governed.

The conviction that political security and progress are made effective by the union of national independence with representative government rests upon a totally defective analysis that was responsible in no small measure for the failure to forecast and to prevent the collapse of 1914. The nature of the flaw in this polity is slow to emerge to the middle-class intelligence, necessarily approaching public affairs with the prepossession of its class. We can best discover it by turning once more to the defects of nationalism. The first we have already indicated, e.g. the masking of the interests or ambitions of a ruling, owning class or caste in the national movement. Nationalism is often internally oppressive. But a second vice bred of struggle and the intensity of self-realization is an exclusiveness which easily lends itself to fiscal or military policies of national defence, through which dangerous separatist interests are fostered within the national State. The spirit of nationalism, stimulated by the struggle for independence, easily becomes so self-centred as to make its devotees reckless of the vital interests of the entire outside world. To Irish Nationalists, Czecho-Slovaks or Poles, this vast world struggle has been apt to figure merely or mainly as their great opportunity for the achievement of a national aim to which they are willing to sacrifice the lives, property and rights of all other peoples without a qualm. This absorbing passion, like others, is exploited for various ends and is the spiritual sustenance of the protectionism that always brings grist to the commercial mill. But there is a third defect which partakes of the nature of excess. Nationalism may become swell-headed and express itself in territorial aggrandizement. Imperialism is nationalism run riot and turned from self-possession to aggression. No modern nation can pursue a policy of isolation. It must have foreign relations, and its foreign policy may become a "spirited" one, passing rashly into schemes of conquest and annexation.

These three perversions of nationalism, the oppressive, the exclusive and the aggressive, are all grounded in the usurpation of a nation by a predominant class or set of interests. This class-power is rooted often in traditional prestige, but this prestige itself rests upon solid economic supports. Landlordism and serfdom, capitalism and wagedom, money-lending and indebtedness—such have been the distinctive cleavages which have so often made a mockery of the boasted national freedom.

If we turn from this survey of nineteenth-century nationalism to a consideration of the democratic movement with which it has been associated, we discover that "democracy" is vitiated by the same defects. It either signifies Parliamentarism upon an utterly inadequate franchise, by which the majority of the governed have no electoral voice, or else the formal government by the people is a machinery controlled for all essential purposes by small powerful groups and interests. Political democracy based upon economic equality is as yet an unattained ideal.

The liberal political philosophers of the Victorian era failed entirely to comprehend this vital flaw in the movement of nationalism and democracy. That failure was chiefly due to their underlying assumption that politics and business were independent spheres. It was in their view as illicit for business interests to handle politics as for government to encroach upon or hamper business interests. Such interference from either side appeared to them unnecessary and injurious. They failed to perceive that the evolution of modern industry, commerce and finance, had two important bearings upon politics. In the first place, it impelled business interests to exercise political pressure upon government for tariff aids, lucrative public contracts, and for favourable access to foreign markets and areas of development. Secondly, it evoked a growing demand for the protection of weaker industries, the workers and the consuming public from the oppressive power of strong corporations and combinations, which in many of the essential trades were displacing competition.

In other words, history was playing havoc with the economic harmonies upon which Bastiat and Cobden relied for the peaceful and fruitful co-operation of capital and labour within the nation, and of commerce between the different countries of the world. Cobden valiantly assailed the militarism, protectionism and imperialism of his day, and recognized their affinity of spirit and certain of their common business aims, but without any full perception of their economic taproot, or of the rapid domination over foreign policy which they were soon destined to attain. The grave social-economic problems which have lately loomed so large in the statecraft of every country lay then unrecognized. Throughout the long public career of two such genuinely liberal statesmen as Cobden and Gladstone neither evinced the slightest recognition that the State had any interest or obligation in respect of health and housing, the wages, hours and tenure of employment, the settlement of issues between capital and labour, or in any drastic reforms of our feudal land system. So far as they recognized these economic grievances at all, they deemed individual or privately associated effort to be the proper and adequate mode of redress. Where government was called upon to intervene for liberative or constructive work, the superficiality of its treatment showed a quite abysmal ignorance of social structure. A generation in which the Artisans' Dwellings Act of 1875, the Ground Game and Small Holdings Act of the early eighties, and the Factory Acts of 1870 and 1878 ranked as serious contributions to a new social policy, is self-condemned for utter incapacity to see, much less to solve, the social problem. Such statecraft failed to perceive that the new conditions of modern capitalist trade and finance had poisoned the policies of nationality and democratic self-government, and were breeding antagonisms that would bring class war within each nation and international war in its train.

Not until the eighties did these antagonisms begin to become evident to those with eyes to see. During the period 1850 to 1880, Britain had still remained so far ahead of other countries in her industrial development, her foreign trade, her shipping and her finance as to entertain no fears of serious rivalry. Though our markets and those of our world-wide Empire were formally open upon equal terms to foreign merchants, our traders held the field, and British enterprise and capital met little competition in European markets or in loans for the great railroad development in North and South America. Not until the industrial countries of the Continent had reconstituted their industries upon British models and had furnished themselves with steam transport, while the United States, recovered from the Civil War, was advancing rapidly along the same road, was any check put upon the optimism which held that England was designed by Providence to be the abiding workshop of the world. Throughout the mid-Victorian era our economists and social prophets, with a few exceptions, were satisfied with a national prosperity and progress which enriched business classes, while the level of comfort among the skilled artisans showed a fairly constant and considerable rise.

Internally the economic harmony appeared, at any rate to well-to-do observers, justified by events. Externally there seemed no reason for suspecting any gathering conflict from the fact that one great nation after another was entering the path of industrial capitalism. Why should the rising productivity and trade of Germany, the United States and other developing nations be any source of enmity or injury to us? The economic harmonies were clear in their insistence that free intercourse would bring about an international division of labour as profitable to all the participating nations as the similar division of labour within each nation was to its individual members. It was impossible for the world to produce too much wealth or too rapidly for the satisfaction of the expanding wants of its customers. Foolish persons prated of over-production and pointed to recurrent periods of trade depression and unemployment. But the harmonists saw nothing in these phenomena but such friction, miscalculation and maladjustment as were involved in the processes of structural change and the elasticity of markets. As a noted economist of the eighties put it, " the modern system of industry will not work without a margin of unemployment."

All the same, several notable occurrences in the eighties ruffled the complacency of the mid-Victorian optimism. One was the revelation of the massed poverty and degradation of the slum-dwellers in our towns, and the searchlight turned upon working-class conditions in this and other lands by the competing criticisms of Henry George and the newly formed socialist organizations. The second was the rise in the United States of those Trusts and other formidable combinations which emerged as the culmination and the cancelment of that competition upon which the harmonists relied for the salutary operation of their economic laws.

The third event did not assume at first sight an economic face. It was the testimony to competing Imperialism furnished by the Berlin Conference for the partition of Central Africa. This was the first intimation to the world of a new rivalry, the true nature of which lay long concealed under the garb of foreign policy, and in the eighties was by no means plain to the statesmen who were its executants.

Imperialism is not, indeed, a simple policy with a single motive. It is compact of political ambition, military adventure, philanthropic and missionary enterprise and sheer expansionism, partly for settlement, partly for power, partly for legitimate and materially gainful trade. But more and more, as the White man's world has been occupied and colonized, the aggrandizing instincts have turned to those tropical and subtropical countries where genuine white colonization is precluded and where rich natural resources and submissive lower peoples present the opportunity of a new and distinctively economic empire.

Since the compelling pressure from this greed of empire has been the main source of the growing discord in the modern world, it is of the utmost importance to understand how the discord rises, and to see its organic relation to the class war within the several nations which has grown contemporaneously with it. If modern industrial society were closely conformable to the economic harmonies, the mobility and competition of capital and business ability would ensure that no larger share of the product was obtained by the owners of those productive agents than served to promote their useful growth and efficiency, and that the surplus of the fruits of industry would pass to the general body of the working population in their capacity of wage-earners and consumers, through the instrumentality of high wages and low prices. Combinations of workers would be needless and mischievous, for they could not increase the aggregate that would fall to labour, and the gains they might secure for stronger groups of workers would be at the expense of the weaker sections. It was to the interest of labour that capital and business ability should be well remunerated, in order that the increase of savings and of the wage-fund should be as large as possible, and that the arts of invention and business enterprise should be stimulated to the utmost. For labour was the residuary legatee of this fruitful co-operation. It was, again, a manifest impossibility that production should outstrip consumption, for somebody had a lien upon everything that was produced and the wants of men were illimitable. Thus effective demand must keep pace with every increase of supply. The notion that members of the same trade were hostile competitors, in the sense that there was not enough market to go round, and that if some sold their goods others would fail to sell, seemed a palpable absurdity.

Yet it was precisely these impossibilities and absurdities that asserted themselves as dominant facts in the operation of modern capitalist business. Every business man knew from experience that a chronic tendency to produce more goods than could profitably be sold prevailed over large fields of industry, that the wheels of industry had frequently and for long periods to be slowed down in order to prevent overproduction, and that more and more work, money, force and skill had to be put into the selling as distinguished from the productive side of a business. Every instructed worker knew that wealth was not, in fact, distributed in accordance with the economic harmonies, that much of it stuck in the form of rent and other unearned or excessive payments for well placed capital and brains, and that the great gains of the technical improvements did not come down to "the residual legatee." Where free competition survived, it became cut-throat, leading to unremunerative prices, congested markets and frequent stoppages: when effective combination took its place, restricted output and regulated prices operated both in restraint of production and in the emergence of monopoly. Put otherwise, the weaker bargaining power of labour, pitted against the superior material resources, organization, knowledge and other strategic advantages of the landowning, capitalist and entrepreneur classes, left the former with an effective demand for commodities too small to purchase the products of the machine industries as fast as these were capable of providing them. The habitual underconsumption of the workers, due to the massing of unearned or excessive income in the hands of the master classes, has been the plainest testimony to the reality of that antagonism of interests within each nation which is dramatized as "class war." No smooth talk about the real identity of interests between capital and labour disposes of the issue. A real identity does exist within certain limits. It does not pay capitalists, employers, landowners or other strong bargainers, to drive down wages below the level of efficiency. Nor does it pay labour, even should it possess the power, to force down "profits" below what is required, under the existing arrangements, to maintain a good flow of capital and technical and business ability into a trade. But, wherever the state of trade is such as to yield a return more than enough to cover these minimum provisions, the surplus is a real "bone of contention," and lies entirely outside the economic harmonies. It goes to the stronger party as the spoils of actual or potential class war. Strikes and lock-outs are not the wholly irrational and wasteful actions they appear at first sight. In default of any more reasonable or equitable way of distributing the surplus among the claimants, they rank as a natural and necessary process. However much we may deplore class war, it is to this extent a reality, and does testify to an existing class antagonism inside our social-economic system.

I have already explained by implication how this inherent antagonism of classes contains the seeds of the wider antagonism of States and governments. The maldistribution of wealth, which keeps the consuming power of the people persistently below the producing power of machine industry, impels the controllers of that industry to direct more and more of their energy to secure foreign markets so as to take the goods they cannot sell at home, and to prevent producers in other countries, confronted with the same necessity, from entering their home market. Here is a simultaneous drive for governmental aid: first in protecting the home market from the invasion of foreign goods; secondly, in inducing or coercing the governments of foreign countries to admit our goods into their market on more favourable terms than those of other competing countries. Hence arise three policies, all pregnant with international antagonism. Protection, adopted primarily in order to secure home trade and keep out the foreigner, is a constant breeder of dissension among peoples and governments. Its secondary effect, to assist strong combinations within a country, to stifle free competition and by imposing high prices to increase the volume of surplus profit, further aggravates that maldistribution of the national income which we recognize as the mother of discord. For this increased surplus means a further restriction of internal consumption and a corresponding pressure for enlarged foreign outlets. More and more must the capitalist classes in each industrially advanced country press their governments for protection at home and a powerful bagman's policy abroad.

Protection, however, is only the first plank in this platform. The second is diplomatic and other pressure brought to bear on weaker States for trading privileges or special spheres of commercial interests, as in China and Persia, or for the enforcement of debt payment or other business arrangements in which private traders or investors demand redress for injuries. This last consideration introduces the third and by far the most important cause of international discord. The surplus income under modern capitalism cannot, it must be recognized, be absorbed in extending the productive machinery needed to supply our home markets. Nor can it find full remunerative occupation in the supply of foreign markets, either under the condition of free competition with exporters from other countries or by such trading privileges as those to which we have alluded. An increasing proportion of that surplus income must be permanently invested in other countries. This has been the most important factor in the economic and political transformation of the world during the last generation. Under the direction of skilled financiers an increasing flow of surplus or savings has gone about the world, knocking at every door of profitable investment and using governmental pressure wherever it was necessary. Special railway, mining or land concessions, loans pressed upon State governments or municipalities, or in backward countries upon kinglets or tribal chiefs, the pegging out of permanently profitable stakes in foreign lands —these methods have been employed by strong business syndicates everywhere with more or less support from their government. Such areas, at first penetrated by private business enterprise, soon acquire a political significance, which grows along a sliding scale of slippery language from "spheres of legitimate aspiration" to "spheres of influence," protectorates and colonial possessions. Now, just as there is not enough home market for goods or capital to take up the trade "surplus," so there is found to be not enough world market for the growing pressure of world capital seeking these outside areas of investment and the markets which go with them. More and more this pressure of financiers for profitable foreign fields has played in with the political ambitions of statesmen to make the inflammable composition of modern Imperialism. This Imperialism is thus seen to be the close congener of the Capitalism and Protectionism that are the roots of class antagonism within the several nations. While it nourishes jealousies, suspicions and hostilities between nations, it also strengthens the master classes in every nation by forging the joint political and economic weapons of Protection and Militarism, and by seeking to cross and so confuse the class antagonism by masquerading as "Nationalism." Quite plainly the imperialist or capitalist says to the worker, "Come in with us in our great imperialistic exploitation of the world. This is the only way of securing the large expanding and remunerative markets necessary to furnish full regular employment at high wages. Come in with us and share an illimitable surplus, got not from underpaying you, but out of the untapped resources of the tropics worked for our joint benefit by the lower races." This invitation to wholesale parasitism is openly flaunted by such bodies as the Imperial Resources Development Committee, and is more timidly suggested in various new projects for harmonizing the interests of capital and labour on the basis of the development of capitalistic combinations. Were it successful, it would do nothing to heal the discord either between capital and labour in this country or between the divergent interests of capitalist groups in the several countries. Nay, even if it were extended by some international concert of Western capitalist-powers to a more or less complete control of the tropics, it would only enlarge the area of discord by arraying the ruling Western nations of the world against the lower races whom they had set to grind out wealth to be taken for the consumption of their masters.

I must not, however, carry further at this stage this speculative glance into the possible future. For what concerns us here is to understand the sources of the blindness which caused the war to break upon us as a horrible surprise. I desire here to show that this blindness lay in a deep-seated misapprehension of the dominant movements of the century, and particularly of the latest outcomes of perverted Nationalism and Capitalism in their joint reactions upon foreign relations.

We have seen these two dominant forces emerging and moulding the course of actual events. Nationalism and Capitalism in secret conjunction produced independent, armed and opposed powers within each country, claiming and wielding a paramountcy, political, social and economic, within the nation, and working for further expansion outside. This competition of what may fairly be called capitalist States, evolving modern forms of militarism and protectionism, laid the powder trains. The dramatic antithesis of aggressive autocracies and pacific democracies in recent history is false, and the failure to discern this falsehood explains the great surprise. Nowhere had the conditions of a pacific democracy been established. Everywhere an inflamed and aggrandizing Nationalism had placed the growing powers of an absolute State (absolute alike in its demands upon its citizens and in its attitude to other States) at the disposal of powerful oligarchies, directed in their operations mainly by clear-sighted business men, using the political machinery of their country for the furtherance of their private interests. This by no means implies that States are equally aggressive, equally absolute, and equally susceptible to business control. Still less does it imply that in the immediate causation of the war conscious economic conflicts of interests were the efficient causes, or that direct causal responsibility is to be distributed equally among the belligerent groups. Indeed, the account of nineteenth-century movements here presented, if correct, explains why the German State became more absolutist in its claims and powers than other States, more consciously aggressive in its external policy, and in recent years more definitely occupied with economic considerations. Its geographical position, its meagre access to the sea, its rapid recent career of industrialism, its growing need of foreign markets, and its late entrance upon the struggle for empire, all contributed to sharpen the sense of antagonism in German statecraft and to make it more aggressive. The pressures for forcible expansion were necessarily stronger in this pent-up nation than in those which enjoyed in a literal sense "the freedom of the seas" and large dependencies for occupation, government, trade priority and capitalistic exploitation. The ruthless realism of German statecraft, its habitual and successful reliance upon military force, the tough strain of feudal tyranny and servitude surviving in the spirit of Prussian institutions, served to make Germany in a quite peculiar degree the centre of discord, alike in its internal and its external polity. In the nation where Marx and Bismarck had stamped their teaching so forcibly upon the general mind, no great faith in the economic harmonies and pacific internationalism could be expected to survive. To these distinctively realistic forces must be added the subtler but not less significant contributions of Hegel and Darwin, working along widely different channels to give a "scientific" support to political autocracy, economic domination and an absolutist State striving to enforce its will in a world of rival States contending for survival and supremacy. Out of that devil's brew were concocted the heady doctrines of Treitschke and his school, to whose educative influences such extravagant importance is attached by those who seek to represent the whole German nation as privy to a long preconcerted plan for war. That large romantic theories, claiming scientific or philosophical authority, have had, especially in Germany, a considerable influence in disposing the educated members of the ruling and possessing classes to accept policies of force in the internal and external acts of government that seemed favourable to their interests and prestige, there can be no doubt. We also know that in Germany and elsewhere, among the class-conscious leaders of socialist and labour movements, a sort of semi-scientific sanction for the use of violence in a class war that was an inevitable phase in the evolution of a "new" society was based upon the same biological misconception.

But we must not be misled by ideologists or heated pamphleteers into imputing an excessive value to these theories regarded as actual forces in conduct. Were this value what it is pretended in some quarters, the war would not have come as a surprise. It would have been expected. The wide prevalence of doctrines of "force," rivalry of nations, and struggles for survival on a basis of social efficiency, were not in any real sense determinant factors in bringing about the war. Nor did they do more than mitigate in more reflecting minds the profound astonishment which accompanied the outbreak of war. The really operative causes were the deep antagonisms of interest and feeling which the analysis has disclosed, or, conversely, the feebleness of the safeguards upon which liberal and humane thinkers had relied, viz. economic internationalism, democracy and the restricted functions of the State.

CHAPTER II

DOWN THE RAPIDS

As we look back upon the period of the war, we seem to see the numerous participant nations falling for the most part into their pre-ordained places by some natural law of their being. Some moved swiftly and as if it were instinctively into their grouping; others, held at first in unstable equilibrium by opposing attractions, slowly or suddenly fell into place. One or two, inert in the earlier years of conflict, by reason of aloofness and size, like the United States, China and certain South American States, were drawn in by later impulsion. In each instance, at the time a great variety of delicate and conflicting considerations appeared to give a character of reasonable choice. But, as we look back upon the movement, these reasons and considerations seem to disappear before some sense of inevitable tendency resembling the operations of physical law. An arresting phrase, used by Sir Edward Grey during the Agadir crisis of 1911, expressed a fear lest France should be "drawn into the orbit of German diplomacy." The unconscious abdication of free-will thus imputed to foreign policy well indicates our feeling as we turn our mind upon the larger political happen-

4

ings, regarded as the product of current forces or tendencies.

But, if this holds of the politics of the war itself, it equally applies to our mental attitude in retrospection of the years immediately preceding 1914. The metaphor, however, is here instinctively shifted from the sphere of molar physics. We see a world tossed down the rapids and racing towards the fall. The perils of these tumultuous years now appear so manifest that we marvel at our blind complacency.

I merely allude in passing to the more obvious external symptoms of the impending break-up of the Great Peace; the race of Armaments, with the organized trade interests behind this costly sport; the incidents of Zabern, Agadir and other sword-brandishing; the rising notes of challenge in patriotic statesmen and inflamed Presses; the grave occurrences in Ireland and India, Armenia, Persia, China and other disturbed areas. Of even deeper significance than these open menaces of war were the forces and issues of the social-economic conflict which broke into a new violence in every civilized country. "Unrest" was everywhere passing into active disturbance. This unrest had its roots in working-class discontent. The working classes in most countries, gathering ever more numerously in large cities, were getting formal and informal education. The knowledge of good and evil, of riches and poverty, was coming home to them. Their felt needs were outstripping their powers of satisfaction. The immensity of the control of man over the productive resources of nature became common knowledge to men employed in modern industry and commerce. Wealth seemed to them illimitable in its growth. But they were getting little, though the human toil fell as heavily as ever on their nerve and muscle. Nay, owing to the play of recent economic forces which they could neither comprehend nor control, they were losing ground in the economic struggle. Rising prices for many years past had been filching from them all and more than they could get by concerted action in raising money-wages.

This holding up of the normal and fairly regular improvement in working-class conditions which, at different paces in different classes and countries, had been taking place so long, is of primary importance in explaining the blind ferment of labour troubles in this pre-war period. The new spirit of exasperation was sharpened by the failure of regular trade-unionism to achieve any redress of their grievance. This failure was inevitable. Such progress as the workers had made in wages and other conditions was mainly due to the operation of competition within the capitalist system. Though competition of businesses within each trade did not, as orthodox political economy pretended, secure for the worker the favoured position of a residuary legatee, to whom every industrial improvement came home in higher real wages, it did safeguard his interests against many forms of exploitation. Now, with the close of the nineteenth century, this era of competition may be said to have ended. In almost all great capitalistic industries and trades, combination was displacing competition in the determination of prices. Trusts, associations, regulation of markets, price agreements, were not new discoveries. They had long been operative influences in restraint of competition. But competition had been the dominant force, combination operating as friction. Now the rôle of the two was reversed. The normal structure of large modern trades was based upon arrangements for combined action; such competition as remained represented the failure to carry combination to completion. With quickening pace this movement proceeded in the closing decade of the nineteenth century and the opening years of this century. It appeared not only in the most highly organized industries, metals, textile, engineering, chemicals, and the like, but in many smaller highly specialized trades whose products were supplementary to some great industry, as in the various combinations which to-day are holding up prices in materials for the building trade. This disappearance or loss of effective competition in industry is of vital importance in an understanding of the new industrial unrest. But associated with it was another economic factor, even more mysterious to the worker, which is sometimes called the Money Power. Without attempting here any close analysis of this portent, we may describe it as an increasing power of financial capitalism, i.e. bankers, financiers and speculators, to operate the marketing and investment systems, so as to make large profits out of manipulations which have the effect of raising prices. The excessive provision of credit facilities, with the result that purchasing power rises faster than the supply of perishable goods, was the chief and most injurious result of this process.

This tightening grip of capitalistic combinations, manifested in the failure of wages to keep pace with rising prices by ordinary process of collective bargaining, drove the trade unions into politics, and was a chief factor in the formation of the Labour

Party. This move exposed the workers to a new propaganda of socialism and syndicalism. To the more conservative trade unionists, labour representation meant only, as they hoped, a more effective means of buttressing trade-union action by legislative supports in the way of minimum wages, eight hours day, unemployment provisions. But the younger and more radical elements began to take on more revolutionary ideas about the status of labour and the supercession of wagedom by some system in which the "proletariat" (new word of ominous significance) should exercise control. At first it seemed plausible that the vote and the electoral machinery could be used to better their conditions and effect this transformation of control. But the experience of the opening decade of this century was one of disillusionment. Political action appeared as impotent as trade-union action in satisfying their demands. Parliamentarism as well as orthodox Trade Unionism was then threatened by a working-class spirit of revolt against established leadership and policy. The younger workers were challenging the old order, alike in industry and politics. Openly contemptuous of the State and its politicians, some of them succumbed to the new doctrine of an industrial government which would run the business side of national life in virtual independence of, or in some quite loose and negligible relation to, the political State. Though this syndicalist teaching, regarded as doctrine, did not spread very widely or go very deep, it supplied an intellectual yeast in the mass of discontent. The revolt against authority and recognized methods of award and settlement in the pre-war strikes was a new and disconcerting note in the labour world.

This stirring of the workers, with its direct menace to property, control of industry and security of comfortable life, was getting on the nerves of the employing, owning and ruling classes. Hitherto, by political and social management, with the arts of inexpensive concession and compromise, they had retained all the substance of their power. But the Parliamentary game, hitherto engaged in giving spurious importance and excitement to issues of tertiary value, was becoming dangerous. The Labour Party was in its present form and force innocuous, but the popular radicalism, of which Mr. Lloyd George became the mouthpiece and executant, contained in its land reforms and its predatory taxation a real source of disquietude. Never since the days of the first Reform Bill were the fears of property so deeply roused. The destruction of the veto of the House of Lords seemed to some "the beginning of the end," the first formal step in a revolution which would depose the government of those with "a stake in the country" and let in the flood tide of democracy. Though the upper and middle classes had long done lip-service to popular government, they had always distinguished that tempered democracy in which they acted for the people, with such "consent" as electoral machinery could easily be made to yield, from the dangerously subversive pressures of popular force upon the levers of government.

Class war in industry and politics, in a word, came in this pre-war period as a reality in thought, feeling and action. The British experience of it was rendered more alarming by the fiercer outbreaks of the same conflict upon the Continent. Italy, France, Germany, Austria, Spain and Scandinavia were all scenes of the same unrest, with strikes and political disturbances of novel nature and intensity. Everywhere the spirit of unreason, passion and force was abroad. In each country the self-protective instinct of the ruling classes set itself to ripen policies which should "stay giddy minds with foreign quarrels." How rapidly this compost of mutual suspicions and irritations was ripening towards class war was most dramatically shown in the Irish trouble of 1913 and 1914. Here an important section of the political and soc al leaders of this country avowed their intention to disobey the law, to violate that Constitution of which they had professed to be the faithful guardians, and to support the Ulster treason-mongers in their forcible resistance to the Home Rule Act. This action cannot be interpreted merely in the light of Irish policy. It was nothing less than an open declaration of aggressive war by the active representatives of the Conservative party against what they regarded as the predatory and revolutionary movement of a proletarian government. It was the 1909 Budget, the destruction of the Lords' Veto, the English Land Campaign, the growing strength of Trade Unionism, the experience of paralysing strikes, that evoked this declaration of the Unionist leaders. The Army was theirs, and they were prepared, now that constitutional supports were failing them, to have resort to its force in the defence of their property and power.

Class war was accompanied by a simultaneous ebullition of sex war. Here Britain was the stage of intensest action. The movement for woman suffrage, hitherto confined to orderly progress by argument and education, suddenly blazed forth into a furious propaganda, accompanied by displays of passionate force which staggered the world. The surprise which greeted this outbreak was due to a failure to give proper recognition to the wider and deeper elements of sex-feeling which found expression in demands for the economic independence of women, equal access to trades and professions, endowment of maternity, reform of the marriage and divorce laws, etc.

This direct challenge to the established status of the family and home, and to the tacit conventions which hitherto had kept women (with rare exceptions) out of public life, is perhaps the best approach to a deeper consideration of the "rapids" down which we were racing. For there are two characteristics of these turbulent years. One is the disposition to break away from the usages, conventions and authorities which had hitherto ruled conduct in most human relations, within the family, the trade, the party, the church, the State. This was not confined to the intellectual classes, and could not therefore be imputed directly to the play of the rationalizing spirit upon its critical side. The decay of religion and a loosening of conventional morality, assuredly a marked feature of the pre-war era, were not to any large degree due to conscious rationalism. Religion was not exposed or refuted, but its hold became feebler, its doctrines and its rites seemed to larger and larger numbers of people unmeaning and out of keeping with modern life. The regular practice of churchgoing, never strong among town-workers, was everywhere dropping away, or, so far as it survived, was losing its old sanction and becoming a social observance. Family prayers, the last relic of religion in the household, was a rare survival even in late Victorian days. In the school, religion lived the attenuated life of a "Scripture lesson." Everywhere, except in a few hectic revivals or in little circles of new sacerdotalism, religion was fading away as an influence in life. The Sabbath had been invaded and routed by the bicycle, golf, the motor-car and "social duties." The long-clinging distinction between Sunday and week-day reading was dissipated by the Sunday Press, and the novel was no longer sinful.

With this weakening of religion went a weakening of some of the older moral obligations. The sense of sin itself, which marked the dependence of morality on religion, was obsolescent, and the entire "puritan" conception of life of which it was the kernel was being eaten away. It was for the most part an insensible change. Just as the dogmas of religion were not openly rejected but became unreal, so with many social conventions. The old autocratic authority of the father and the husband in the home: the relation of master and pupil in modern school life: of employer and employed in the typical modern business —in every department of human relation important changes affecting personality had been taking place. Some of them had definitely affected "morals." Those forms of wrongdoing classed as crimes were not upon the increase, nor can it be asserted that society as a whole was becoming more immoral in the sense of wilful injury to others or definite breaches of the accepted code. But there was certainly a more lenient attitude towards sexual irregularities and an increasing laxity in business life. In general there was, I think, freer vent for selfishness and a lack of self-restraint in all matters of the appetite.

It may be urged that these are slower changes of a general character which belong to the last generation and of no special applicability to "the rapids." And this in some sense is true. But the turbulent happenings in politics and industry during these last years brought an acceleration of these changes. Moreover, there is one important factor to be taken into account—the reaction of recent mechanical inventions upon the general mind. The opening of the twentieth century marked the transition from the steam age to the electric age. This was accompanied by the swift popularization of a number of inventions. The telephone, the motor-car, the cinema, the aeroplane, the gramophone had staggered the popular imagination with a sense of the miraculous. They had transformed the material environment for millions of people, and had imposed novel interests so numerous and so exciting as to produce nervous disturbances which contributed not a little to the general atmosphere of unrest.

This great new burst of mechanical inventions, entering into the lives of the people, coincided with and contributed to a general advance of material prosperity among the upper and middle grades of society. Luxury and extravagance were everywhere in open evidence. The motor-car advertised a new class distinction, and gave a deceptive multiplication to the numbers of the "idle rich." Sports and recreation, social functions and all the apparatus of pleasure, took on new forms of wildness and passion. The renovated zest for prize-fighting vied in popular interest with the earlier ventures in the conquest of the air, and an orgy of wild eccentricity in dancing seized all classes of society. The world, indeed, went dancing to the very brink of the abyss.

It seems as if this riot of luxury and corybantism were a protective dope of insensibility, prompted by some instinctive premonition of the catastrophe.

Not only dancing, but all the arts of music, painting, the drama, poetry were invaded by a rush of violence and passion, bursting the accepted moulds and finding new restless and impulsive modes of expression. The extremes of realism and of mysticism, passionate asceticism cheek by jowl with unbridled license, broke out in all the arts. In music and painting the repudiation of prevailing standards and conventions was most marked. The ruthless audacities of post-impressionism, futurism, cubism, symbolism were the announcement of a world breaking away from all settled laws of life and plunging into chaos. For the distinctive appeals of these new forms of art were not, as sometimes pretended, to a superior sincerity of feeling, accuracy of perception or truth in rendering, but to the passion of violence and a free abandonment to the emotion of the moment or to sheer eccentricity.

Force took the place of beauty, quick suggestion of firm presentation. Everywhere was a contemptuous rejection of the past and its valuations. In line, colour and subject, violence was the prevailing note, with an extravagant distortion of the plain records of nature. In music there appeared the same abandonment of smooth and intelligible rhythm and harmony, and a cult of jerks, swerves and dissonances. *Vers libras* with its obtrusion of " unpoetical " topics in startling or slatternly guise, and swift plunges into the uglier sensualities or their related mysticisms, was a marked literary feature of the pre-war era. A certain sympathy between this art and the revolutionary teaching of such theorists as Sorel, with his doctrine of force-generating myths, was evident, their common character consisting in the glorification of violence and disorder as intrinsic value for "red-bloods."

In the realm of deeper thought this movement took shape in a vigorous reaction against rationalism and the scientific conception of continuity in evolution. Everywhere new stress was laid upon discontinuous mutations, the creative, the explosive, the unpredictable. The reduction of scientific laws to working hypotheses, whose validity is constantly subject to revision and displacement by hypotheses which "work" better, had for some time past been sapping popular confidence in the absolutism of science. Upon the top of this came Pragmatism, with its repudiation of the scientific assumption of a single intelligible system, breaking up the universe into a multiverse, and setting the new psychology to work at destroying the claim of scientific men to reach "objective" truths through "hard" facts. Bergson, with his sceptical analysis of the instrument of reason and his *élan vital,* made a profound impression upon the educated classes in the various European nations. The Freudian psycho-analysis, spreading like wildfire among continental intellectuals, had already begun to reach this country and to complete the demolition of the claim of man to be a reasoning animal. Science and reason were to be put in their proper place as tools for the creative soul of man, whose pulsing instincts, emotions, intuitions and desires were the real determinants of human conduct (including the discovery and systematization of knowledge) and were inciting us to mould the physical and spiritual universe according to our hearts' desire. If this appeared too anthropomorphic a creed, this same creative urge of life was extended to other orders of organic and inorganic matter, a creative evolution of the whole. But in this philosophy, as in the art, the politics, the personal ethics of the era, the same essential character showed through, viz. a repudiation of reason, regularity, authority, continuity, harmony, and a reliance upon instinct and spontaneity. The churches began to dabble in this philosophy as yielding new buttresses to "faith" and authority; revolutionary theorists gladly incorporated a special rendering of it for their destructive adventures. I am not here concerned to assess the soundness of the psychology on which this new "philosophy" was built, but only with its immediate intellectual and emotional reactions. The teaching was absorbed in a thousand circles where serious thinking had always been taboo; it seized, I will not say the popular fancy, but the fancy of large educated strata who previously had not known philosophy could be made "interesting." In other words, it furnished a reputable support for the irrationalism, the violence, the recklessness which economic discontent, luxurious dissipation, collapse of religion, pushful politics, nerve-straining mechanical inventions, had loosened to drive a blind world down the swirling rapids to the fall.

PART II

THE CIVILIAN MIND

CHAPTER I

THE SPIRIT OF THE HERD

THE war has been " a school of character " in more than one sense. Its " bracing experience " shook the upper classes of our people out of the mood of reckless hedonism which insecure prosperity engendered, and drew out their rich endowments for adventure and leadership. It sobered the fractious unrest of the workers, laid the rising passion of " a class struggle," and inspired a fresh sentiment of national unity. The continuous efforts and sacrifices of whole peoples, consciously devoted to the achievement of a national end of novel and transcendent value, seemed to disclose and educate new powers of unselfish co-operation capable of achieving great and lasting improvements in the character and conduct of society. The war showed that our wealthy leisured classes were not so sunk in luxury and ease, our business men not so immersed in selfish greed, our working classes not so reckless of the commonweal, the nation as a whole not so abandoned to materialism and intellectual inefficiency, as their enemies and some of their censorious friends had depicted them. The tough fibre, the indomitable courage and endurance, the high adaptability and power of initiative, the comradeship, which our fighting men displayed on land, at sea, in air, our civil population also showed in meeting the strains of war upon their spiritual and physical resources. Our powers to improvise and "carry on," in the formation and equipment of our new forces, in the conduct of industries, the economy of our consumption and notably in the organization of the numerous home services, exceeded all our expectations. In dispelling the notion that we had become a soft, a frivolous, a luxurious and in general a "decadent" nation, the war may thus be said to have re-established our moral self-confidence, if indeed this process was necessary. We now recognize that our stock still retained unimpaired those capacities and energies of body and mind which have enabled us as a nation to play so great a part in history. This recognition probably suffices for the careless many who, contented with this supreme example of our power to rise to an emergency, would return, learning nothing more, to the loose pre-war life of business and amusement. But those who know how near our country came to irretrievable disaster at several junctures, owing to lack of the finer qualities of intelligence and judgment in our generalship and statecraft, are dismayed at the self-complacency which would stake the national existence upon this rough capacity to meet emergencies by improvising remedies for dangers which better mental and moral discipline would have averted.

Edith Cavell's famous saying, "Patriotism is not enough," [1] has not only an extensive but an intensive

[1] It deserves attention that upon the miserable monument to the memory of this heroic woman erected in St. Martin's Lane the banal phrase "For King and Country" is selected to stigmatize her act of sacrifice.

application. To convert raw energy and general good will into national efficiency under high pressure in the face of the enemy is a perilous and expensive process. It was not achieved in any high degree. Certain admitted qualities of spirit and endurance inherent in our stock no doubt counted towards success, but history will attest that in the end it was numbers and volume of land and sea forces that overwhelmed the enemy and secured victory. No doubt we did wonders in military and economic improvisation, taking in slack and making up for lost time. But the revelation of the amount of slack to be taken up, of lost time to be made up, was a scathing commentary on our happy-go-lucky ways and upon the state of mind which underlay them. Sharp criticism had for some time been directed at the defects of our educational system, the lack of science in our industries, the inelasticity of our commercial methods, the short-range opportunism of our statecraft in all departments. The charges were not denied. But they made little impression. For they fell upon a mind which was impenetrable. They were all counts in a single charge of lack of seriousness. To tell us tha as a nation we were not interested in ideas, not willing to devote much time or energy to mental discipline and the pursuit of knowledge, that science, art and literature were regarded as mere ornaments of life, that the very word "culture" carried a flavour of contempt—with such chiding we had been familiar from the time of Matthew Arnold and John Ruskin. We did not repudiate the charge, we rather prided ourselves upon it. We could get on, we did get on, very well without culture. We did not want, did not require, to be "serious" in the sense of undergoing close mental or moral discipline. We did not deny the attractions of the arts and sciences. We could afford to keep, and liked to keep, persons, whole classes of persons, who were "good at that sort of thing." But that the general body of our people, or even of the "educated" classes, should take education and personal culture so seriously as to put them on a higher level of importance than money-making or sports, or even politics, could not be entertained. In no civilized country is "the intellectual life" appraised so low as in England. The other day I met a bright young Englishman who had quite recently returned from Baku, where he had been in business for some years. Talking of the young Russians, he told me in a tone of good-humoured contempt how they would always ask, as their first question about any man he mentioned to them, "Is he intellectual?" He cited instances of young workmen who spoke three or four languages, described the extraordinary development of university teaching among all classes, and told how in dirty little taverns you could hear classical music admirably played on the violin. "They were not," he said, "a practical people"!

Some persons supposed that it might be possible to use the war emergencies as opportunities for widening our intellectual outlook, not so much on the side of disinterested culture as of a wider interpretation of "the practical." The business of the future was going to be built upon applied chemistry, physics and biology: close study of languages, commercial geography, economics and psychology were essential in the struggle for world markets: the elements of mathematics were required for the nicer statistical calculations which underlay "cost-ings," price-curves, finance, insurance and other vital factors in big business operations. Chambers of Commerce talked of encouraging the teaching of Spanish and of Russian, so as to capture German trade, and manufacturers proposed a concession to the utility of scientific experts. War disclosures and emerging business opportunities contributed much to the new push in secondary education. The war had shown us England falling behind in the struggle for trade and wealth, England unequal to her new opportunities, because she was not training properly. Then our higher educationalists gently reminded the practical business man that his utilitarian fruits cannot be grown without a nidus of general culture, with allusions to the failure of a short-cut technical instruction floated upon "whisky money." Our practical man is brought to recognize that there may be something in it, and so he strikes with the educationalist one of those typical British bargains, by which an early addiction to the business life shall be qualified by interludes of learning, conducted in such a way as to preserve intact the supremacy of business over humanity.

Now, in citing this contempt of the ordinary Englishman for "ideas," and even for the higher cultivation of the mind which goes with them, I am not forejudging the issue. The dislike and distrust of the scholar, the thinker, the scientist, *littérateur* and æsthete are in part a protest of "healthy animalism" against the excesses of anæmic intellectualism. The Athenian recognized no such opposition because his education was based upon a just harmony of the claims of body and mind and an organic co-operation of faculties. Modern education in the Western world is slowly groping back to such a harmony, seeking to undo the overspecialism and aloofness of the intellectual life. But there is another ground for the suspicion of culture among the mass of our countrymen. It relates to the esoteric and exclusive standards of intellectual values assigned to studies, tastes and achievements as the decorative hall-marks of a superior class endowed with wealth and leisure. As Mr. Veblen has pointed out in his memorable analysis of the standards of a leisured class, the display of honorific disutility, as testimony to the power to lead an idle predatory life, plays an important part in making and maintaining the hierarchy of values in the education and the culture of our higher social grades The obstinate defence of dead languages as the general key to culture and the equally significant neglect of our own great literature are but one leading case in this elaborate misvaluation.

No small share, therefore, of the habitual disparagement of the life of ideas and the pursuit of knowledge and the fine arts among all classes of Englishmen belongs to the defective presentation of this higher life. The interests of the body and the mind have been too sharply severed, and a narrow pragmatism has vied with a disdainful ornamentalism in blinding us to a just appreciation and cultivation of " the humanities."

. . . . .

It may be said that this is not a state of mind induced by war. True, but war has given it a clearer significance. For it opened out as never before the dangers to which the " practical " man, with his distaste for the life of cultivated thought and feeling, is exposed in a world where the struggle for physical survival is liable to turn more and more upon accurate knowledge, exact thinking, inspired imagination and sympathetic interpretation of human motives. Rude, unformed, wasteful energy counted most heavily in the rough and tumble world that has passed away. Now conscious, calculated policies are demanded in all those departments of life in which the struggle for survival and success is carried on. A people with little aptitude for thought and the laborious acquisition of knowledge, with little curiosity about other people and little sympathy and understanding of their ways, must go under. This problem of better adaptation to the modern environment is "up" to us more closely than to any other people. For our economic and political tentacles reach out more widely and variously over the world than those of any other people.

But this call for intellectual adaptability depends for its response upon appeals to individual personality. No claims for social efficiency can be liquidated in any other way. And it is precisely at this point that we find ourselves most deeply concerned for the self-revelations of the civilian war-mind. For the war has thrown many penetrating shafts of light upon our personality. We have generally held ourselves to be a particularly tough-minded people, fond of personal liberty, making up our mind and doing things our own way, resentful at other people trying to tell us how we ought to think and feel and act in matters lying in the ample field of our private judgment. We have had a pride in "keeping ourselves to ourselves" more than other people, and have been "protestant" as regards the right of forming our own opinions in religion, politics and other areas of debate. Our democracy, we held, was founded more strongly than that of other nations upon the rock of personal liberty alike in thought and action. "Give me to think, to utter and to argue freely, according to conscience, before all other liberties." Other democracies were formed more upon the sense and practice of equality, a higher sentiment of sociality led them to "swarm" more abundantly, and by so swarming to assimilate in thought and feeling and to set less value upon the distinctive individuality of their members. This, we were often told, held of democracy both in France and in the United States: the equality of such peoples was intolerant of personal eccentricities unless they assumed the recognized forms of "genius" or became the decorative badges of heroic leadership. From De Tocqueville to Lord Bryce a series of foreign students had cited as the most distinctive features of American society "the tyranny of the majority" and "the fatalism of the multitude," not confined to the administration of public affairs but penetrating into the inmost recesses of domestic life and private conduct. Even if this conformity were in some sense a voluntary process, that fact did not impair the contrast with a people like ours, who prided themselves upon a certain almost fractious temper of nonconformity, a distaste for smooth unanimities. It may perhaps be urged that I overstress the conscious liberalism and individualism of Britain, ignoring the compelling power of law and custom, prestige and fashion, to mould the mind and conduct of the great mass of contented and inert citizens. But even these conformities, marked as they are by class and local distinction, are seen to be so numerous and various as to relieve the national area from any close uniformity of pattern, while the schismatic tendency, with its right to think and act for oneself, continued operative in every field, from religion to dress.

Now, the great revelation of the war has been the shallow-rootedness of this individualism, with its liberty of private judgment, its scepticism of authority, its resistance of fanaticism, its toleration of differences, that proud and cold reserve which evoked the saying that "every Englishman is an island." Before the impact of war these barriers of unique personality easily collapsed. The collapse was sometimes called patriotism, sometimes national unity. It was a peculiarly British experience in its intensity. Every one of the other belligerent nations, of course, exhibited the same enthusiastic unity, the same intolerance of the tiny refractory minority that dared question the utter rightness of its country's cause. But there was nothing strange in their case. Germany had ironed the intelligence, the emotions and the will of all her citizens into an almost perfect smoothness by her military and educational discipline. The secret nursing of her vengeance, the unavowed but ever dominant *motif* of her public policy, loosed a tide of passion which swept France from end to end with resistless force. Italian "irredentism," stretching into endless vistas of empire, seized and possessed the common mind of the Italian people with a mixed passion of greed and glory. Each of the Balkan States had long lived on the same fare of covetousness disguised as historic rights. The great mass of the Russian population had never emerged from the common life which the uniformity of natural environment and social institutions had stamped upon them into any marked degree of free personality. Neither the feeling of personal liberty nor the habit of private judgment in religion or politics was planted so firmly in any other European country as in England.

Yet the first year of war uprooted the habits of centuries and the sentiments that fed them. At the call of national defence the fierce dissensions of internal politics and industry died down: citizens of every rank hastened to place their lives at the disposal of the State and responded with alacrity to all demands upon their purses and their personal energies. The State was allowed to assume a virtually unlimited control of trade and industry. Innumerable restrictions upon the ordinary comforts, conveniences, and even the necessaries of life were borne with docility or cheerfulness, as the pressure of war tightened. There was a time when, according to good authorities, prohibition of the use of alcoholic drinks would have been accepted. The organized workers were induced without much difficulty to surrender the most cherished safeguards of their economic liberties. When the Government demanded in the name of Defence of the Realm an unlimited right to set aside, by administrative order, or by the mere fiat of a military officer, the ordinary liberties of trade, speech, press and meeting, cancelled *Habeas Corpus* and the right of trial by jury authorized domiciliary visits of the police with the use of *agents provocateurs* and a censorship of letters, telephones and other modes of communication, these demands were met with a wholly uncritical acceptance by all classes. Neither in Parliament nor in the Press nor even in private circles was there any disposition to question or discuss the utility or the necessity of these extraordinary measures. On the contrary, any attempt to discuss them was resented as disloyalty. The very men who had quite recently denounced most vehemently the intelligence and public virtue of the leading figures of the War Government now insisted upon an abject and unquestioned obedience to their every behest.

I am not here concerned to discuss the wisdom or necessity of these war-measures, but to examine the state of mind to which their uncritical acceptance testifies. For while some of these restraints upon individual liberty were evidently needed for the fighting of the war, others may have been unnecessary and others detrimental. But the fact that all were received with equal acquiescence and obeyed with almost equal docility is significant. For it indicates that the critical mind everywhere failed to function. Though it cannot be said that anyone truly believed the Government to be all-wise and all-just, almost everyone behaved as if he did. It is to this point of behaviour that we must direct our mind, if we are to understand what took place. For what is manifest is a rapid collapse of individual thought, feeling and judgment into the condition which is designated a herd-mind. We need not here consider the accuracy of a term which is sometimes taken to mean that the private mind of the individual has been displaced by a collective or aggregate mind. It is sufficient to recognize that individual minds which used to work with great diversity now work with close similarity, and that the new way of working appears to be not a mere averaging if compromising of the old ways, but an inhibition to those activities of the mind in which personal varieties are prevalent and a predominance of those activities in which minds are most alike. There may be something more than this. A sense of common danger and common fear may set up a contagion of feeling which becomes an actual contact, causing what were separate minds to huddle, swarm or fuse in such a manner that emotions or beliefs relating to the object of fear, or the common measures for avoiding it, are communicated with great facility from any one mind to any other. But in whichever way the experience is envisaged it comes to much the same thing. Minds that used to work differently now work similarly, and they all work on some lower plane of resemblance by suspending operations on the higher plane of differences.

This is the beginning of a psychological analysis of national unity. The physical safety of the herd, tribe or other community calls for close, intense, quick and uncritical co-operation. This is procured by a voluntary suspension of those activities of thought and feeling which appear to preclude or impede such co-operation. I spoke of the suspension as voluntary, but acquiescent is perhaps the better term, for the process is for the most part a quiet unconscious abandonment of the higher and more differentiated activities of the mind. In fact, a humorous aspect of the situation arises from the unconsciousness of mental change. For this lapse into the herd-mind involves a reduction of the reasoning faculty to a servitude to the passion of the herd. What the herd-mind craves to believe for the stimulation of its fighting power the reason must find grounds for believing. Where some biologically serviceable belief or notion is generated almost spontaneously out of the passionate imagination of the herd, the business of reason is to lie low and let the belief have a free run. Such was the case with countless stories which found ready credence in all grades of society, of spies and secret signalling, of concrete emplacements, of mutilated nurses, of Russian forces passing through this country, of angels at Mons and the like. The point is not that these stories were false—a few of them were not—but that they seemed to gain credence irrespective of the evidence adduced to support them or their inherent probability. Abject credulity was the foremost quality of the civilian war-mind.

CHAPTER II

VAINGLORY AND CREDULITY

WHEN a schoolboy on first reading Homer finds his heroes on the battlefield bragging before gods and men of their personal prowess and courage and the righteousness of their cause and heaping abusive epithets upon the enemy, it seems to him "bad form" and a bit ridiculous as well. As he grows more familiar and sympathetic with the *naïveté* of the primitive mind, this feeling passes away, and a certain charm attaches to these simple utterances of natural emotion. It is only in the third move that we appreciate the essential humour of the situation. It consists in the unconscious and confident parade of our secret passions as authentic and disinterested standards of objective values. This is everywhere and always the staple of the human comedy. It has grown with civilization and is bred of its bone. For civilization has been continually engaged in repressing this natural tendency of a strong personal bias to usurp the throne of judgment and to pose as objective truth. It is partly for the sake of peace and order that civilized society forbids us openly to dilate upon our own merits and the defects of those whom we dislike, and partly out of a growing regard for stricter and juster judgments than are thus provided.

This social censorship of naïve emotional confessions is, as Freud has well indicated, a condition of the play of the comic spirit in the fields of wit and humour. Chaff, satire, badinage, in particular, are ingenious modes of dodging the censor and winning outlets for our suppressed personal feelings about ourselves and other people. But the very ingenuity of such displays, by introducing an element of self-consciousness, impairs the simple self-deception which is the deeper nature of humour. For the sharp contradiction between what a man is thinking or doing and what he believes himself to be thinking or doing depends on the sincerity of the man's belief. That is why hypocrisy is not humorous save in a merely superficial way. For the conscious pretender fills us with disgust, and so destroys the sympathy upon which the sentiment of humour depends. If a Tartuffe or a Chadband amuses us, it is because the general presumption in favour of truth is so strong that their exaggerated professions of virtue for the moment half-deceive us into thinking them genuine, as children half-believe the most preposterous pretensions of their games. The real comedy lies in disillusionment, in the sudden confrontation of fancies with the facts of life. Perhaps the most poignant form of comedy is the sudden exhibition of the falsehood of our self-appreciation. For most of our disparagement of other people is not gratuitous malice. It is incidental to the process of trying to think and feel ourselves to be better than we really are. We run ourselves up by running others down.

Now, Homeric heroes openly boosted themselves by blackening their enemies. Presumably they felt better and braver after doing so: the rite had "survival value." But a man who does this sort of thing in civilized society is a "bounder," an object of contempt and ridicule. Nevertheless, the old primitive desire to do this very thing remains, and seeks ways of getting round the social censor. It usually finds a way for this self-boosting by collective action. He may talk "heroically" about his school, his party, his country, and disparage other schools, parties and countries, though he knows and everybody knows that he did not choose his school, party or country, and that, if he had happened to belong to any other, his valuations would have been reversed.

Patriotism (or should we not say "patrioteering"? gives the finest field for this play of the comic spirit. For there the self-boosting which provides itself with this collective wrapping presents itself as a lofty and disinterested duty. We ought to feel proud of our country and to feed this pride by talking "big" about it and belittling other countries in comparison. We ought to read all history, past and present, in the light of this obligation, seeing our own country in the centre of the picture, valuing evidence and interpreting events in a favourable light. But, if we are patriots, we ought to feel, while we are doing this, that we are not falsifying facts. The essence of patriotism consists, indeed, in believing somehow, not pretending to believe, that the glorification of our country (with ourselves as the secret core) is consistent with a truthful and dispassionate assessment of evidence. The feeling "My country true or false" would spoil the patriotism. It would also spoil the comedy, by introducing the factor of conscious dishonesty. The genuineness of the conviction that your country is absolutely right, your enemy absolutely wrong, and that your judgment in this matter is absolutely reliable, being founded on a full and fair consideration of all the evidence, is essential to the process.

Civilian life in such a war as that through which we have been passing has been a priceless and unique opportunity for these displays of the comic spirit. The fighting men are too immersed in the hard facts to play illusionizing tricks with them. It is the spectatorial mind and its curious caperings and attitudinizing that give us our material. Psychologists speak of the herd-mind as set up by intensity of common fear or other emotion, and obliging everyone to feel together, think together, act together, for the common safety or the attainment of some other common vital purpose. Now, the subjugation of the separate personality, with its emotional self-control, its more or less disinterested desire for truth, its habit of testing evidence and forming reasonable judgments, to the mastery of the herd-mind is particularly interesting and amusing where minds of high personal culture are involved. For the average sensual man does so little real thinking, and his emotions stand at so primitive a level, that the inflamed irrationality of the war-mind there involves no great sacrifice of personality.

The comedy is enacted among men and women of refined natures and cultivated understandings. The unconscious surrender of so many "educated" persons to the ravages of the herd-mind in the years of war has been a disconcerting exhibition of the instability of the higher qualities of personality. Bottomless credulity, insane suspicion, blazing hatred, unashamed brutality, were exhibited by the gentlest natures. But the most distinctive and widespread trait was the naïve vainglory which was the characteristic of the primitive fighting man, accompanied by all his antics of self-praise and vituperation of the enemy, elaborated to fit the modern circumstances. In ordinary times, an English gentleman who persisted in explaining to all his friends what an excellent fellow he was, how public-spirited and wholly disinterested his conduct, how high-minded his intentions, and what a black-hearted, treacherous villain his enemy was, how cruel, greedy and unscrupulous, and who ended by applauding his own sense of justice and his modesty, would soon become a " butt " to his club companions and acquaintances. The more he produced of his selected facts to support his self-appraisal and the more he insisted upon the impartiality of his presentment the more ridiculous he would make himself. Yet this is precisely what the herd-mind of war-patriotism stampeded us into doing. No sooner did it seize us than the howling dervishes of the Press proclaimed " the holy war," and all our intellectual and spiritual leaders ranged themselves in bands to testify, each in its proper manner, to the truth and justice of the herd's cause and the utter falsehood of all opposing pleas. Truth, usually so hard to find in the tangled affairs of men, became at once transparent; moral responsibility, so difficult to gauge and to distribute, became for this occasion only simplicity itself. Our clergy were genuinely shocked at the blasphemy of the enemy in claiming that " the holy war " was theirs, whilst all the time the hypocrites knew that it was ours. Our philosophers were quick to trace the poison of materialism and absolutism lurking even in the text of Kant; our men of letters found even in Goethe the wicked " will-to-power "; our scientists had long detected the essential barrenness of Germany for big creative ideas, finding her a nest of pilfering adapters;[1] our historians with quick pen redrew modern world-history in black and white. This war was so different from every other war. In others the issues were confused, the motives mixed; here everything was plain and certain to every honest mind. The herd-mind of the enemy stampeded their intellectual and moral leaders into identical postures. The "easy virtue" of the most scrupulous scholars and scientists of every nation, conspiring to uphold the patriotic case presented to them by their several Governments, is an interesting record in war psychology. "Theirs not to reason why," theirs to line up for intellectual and moral support behind the fighting forces of their country. A veritable triumph of Pragmatism, this instinctive attestation of truth as beliefs which help to win the war! The eager industry with which the intellectuals of the contending herds fed them with this war-truth furnishes a valuable commentary on the subjectivity of knowledge.

This feeding has gone on so long that our intellectual digestion has become well adapted to the diet. The Russian news of the year 1919 affords a serviceable test. Although we were well aware that the Russian news served out to us was censored and selected, that contradiction of it, were it false, would be precluded, and that only sources favourable to the accepted policy were tapped, we found it quite easy to assimilate all the stories of revolting cruelty, appalling anarchy and impending collapse charged against the Bolshevik administration by

[1] For a post-war instance of this unconscious humour, cf. the Introduction to Mr. W. McDougall's *The Group-Mind.*

its enemies. We no longer regard impartiality or opportunity of cross-examination as necessary safeguards in the search for political truth. In such material the "will to believe" replaces all other canons.

In a war for truth and justice, justice suffers the same change as truth. Just as truth is what helps to win the war, so justice is the terms imposed by the conquerors. That being so, we recognize that this is a just peace. So M. Clemenceau, Mr. George and even Mr. Wilson assert. The ordinary mind, I think, never having studied Plato, or heard of Thrasymachus, takes what it regards as a common-sense view of justice, consisting in the application of two tests. First, it assumes that the wickedness of "the enemy" is so great that any sort or size of injuries inflicted on him, or his posterity, falls short of his "deserts." Secondly, it accepts as a working definition of justice doing to another as you think he would have done to you. In the application of these tests, they brush aside all scruples about the innocent suffering for the sins of their rulers. And this gives a very interesting instance of the "herd-mind" that dominates them. To their thinking there are not any innocent Germans, because they have lost the power of individualizing. There is not a German, but only "the Germans." Therefore, when you press the blockade after the enemy has surrendered, you are not starving particular German children and old folk (though these die), but only bringing pressure upon Germany. So it seemed natural, and just, early in the war to beat and plunder shopkeepers with German names in reprisal for barbarous acts done by German soldiers or sailors. It was the sentiment of collective responsibility usurping the judgment throne, the herd sense of justice. Critical observers may complain that this attitude is inconsistent with the charge of military autocracy in Germany, to destroy which we went to war. Such an autocracy, they argue, is the negation of real collective responsibility. But there is a separate humour in the notion that you can pin down the herd-mind by the canon of contradiction. The herd-mind recognizes no such law. It is a swivel-mind, easily adjustable to any point of view that is convenient. It has its sophists who will reconcile collective responsibility with autocracy by telling you that servility involves consent. But it does not really need logical defences, for it is pre-logical, or, if you will, a-logical. In the herd-mind, justice is synonymous with unmeasured retribution inflicted on the rival herd. It is not "an eye for an eye." There is no real question of measure or of kind.

And here we approach the core of humour in the comedy of Paris, the savage herd-mind arraying itself in the ceremonial robes appropriate to civilized justice, like a naked Polynesian parading in top-hat and spats. It began with the solemn appointment of a Commission of the leading Allied and Associated Powers to make an impartial inquiry into the question of responsibility for the war, and it ended in the Article of the Peace Treaty setting up "a special tribunal" to try "William II of Hohenzollern, formerly German Emperor, for a supreme offence against international morality and the sanctity of treaties." Who is to try this charge against "international morality"? An international court composed of presumably impartial neutrals? Not so. The court is to be composed entirely of the Kaiser's enemies, who are to be at once prosecutors, judges and executioners. The law, the facts, the verdict and the penalty are al to be found by the complainants, who have already openly and repeatedly committed themselves to the guilt of the defendant. Yet listen to the solemn asseveration of his own high-mindedness and equity by Mr. Justice Lynch: "In its decision the tribunal will be guided by the highest motives of international policy, with a view to vindicating the solemn obligations of international undertakings and the validity of international morality." And in a court so constituted Mr. Lloyd George dared to say "They will get a fair trial, all of them—an absolutely fair trial." He added that "We have got to show that we are a civilized people" and that this is a way of showing it. If this were sheer hypocrisy, disgust would banish humour. But the essential comedy lies in the innocence of those who utter and those who accept these stout assertions of our fitness to be judges in our own case.

CHAPTER III

THE HYSTERIA OF INTOLERANCE

AN even more significant factor in the degradation of the civilian war-mind than its vainglory and credulity is its intolerance. The slow secular struggle for liberty of opinion and expression and of conduct in all essentially self-regarding matters, was commonly supposed to have been won for civilized peoples. In our own country the substantial victory is implied in the later nineteenth-century vindications of freedom by J. S. Mill and Lord Morley. Toleration, and something more than toleration, the energetic stimulation of new and therefore unorthodox opinions, were recognized as the primary condition of all progress and the necessary safeguard for the vitality of all accepted truths. The substance of political as of religious toleration was at any rate believed to have been embodied so securely in our common attitude of mind and institutions that it could not be moved. Britain and America, at any rate, stood for these primary rights of individuality, the right to "think, to utter and to argue freely, according to conscience."

This basis of mental sanity involves, of course, the permission to form and utter opinions which are held to be erroneous and even dangerous by the majority, and which in fact may be obnoxious to both charges. The right to think wrongly, and freely to express such error, is justly held to be essential to the process of selection and rejection by which truth is evolved. It may well be admitted that the strong prejudices of the uneducated masses have never allowed a full response to this claim of fair play, and it has often been contended that even among the more educated strata of society the apparent toleration accorded to unpopular opinions in religion or politics is little more than indifference. This contention, however, we hold to be unwarranted. Making due allowance for a certain impatience felt among intellectual people for what they deem rash heresies or perverse misunderstandings, a fair standard of intellectual toleration was established, based upon a recognition that the method of "trial and error" demanded it.

It is the sudden abandonment during the war of this primary principle of all truth-seeking that is the crucial test of mental degradation. That learned societies should decide permanently to extirpate all enemy membership and influence, that the governing bodies of colleges and other places of higher learning should, on grounds of political or religious opinion, exclude from their teaching staff persons whom they had placed in these posts for their fitness, in order to replace them by presumably less fit teachers, in subjects unrelated either to religion or to politics, is perhaps the most decisive of all evidences of the havoc of the war-mind. It is less the malignity than the irrelevancy of such a mind that obtrudes. Here are persons administering a public trust who think it their duty to deprive the beneficiaries of that trust of certain of its benefits so as to vent the spirit of intolerance which they have dressed up in the garb of patriotism.

When one regards the perpetrators of such intolerant acts from the standpoint of personal responsibility, their conduct seems to merit a degree of moral reprehension which, however, is greatly modified when it is recognized that their personality has been submerged so that they know not what they do. Humorous pity then replaces indignation. These men are no longer the "grave and reverend seigniors" they still appear to themselves, employing their trained judgments in the responsible performance of their duties. They are the instruments of a common passion which has levelled their minds to the plane of the unlettered mob, to whose conduct they conform.

There is, however, a sort of mind standing, or floating, midway between the academic and the popular mind that deserves some separate attention. It is the weathercock or gadfly mind of journalism. How far it reflects, how far creates and feeds, the herd-mind, it is not easy to determine. But one thing is certain. It lives upon that mind, and in order to do so is constantly engaged in moulding it. "What the public wants" means what the herd-mind can assimilate in news, opinions, judgments. To supply this is what the modern newspaper is "for" at all times. For the herd-mind is not merely a war-product. It exists in peace, and the popular Press is its parasitic servant. But in ordinary times the play of independent personality and the faculty of criticism superimposed upon the herd-mind put limits on the journalist. Although as one of our wisest modern commentators has observed, "the Press is a perpetual engine for keeping discussion on a low level," there is some bottom to the presumption of credulity in presenting news, and even a low level of discussion obeys some canons of consistency and decency. But in wartime these checks and limitations are remitted, with a result exceedingly favourable to the power of this Press. An atmosphere of suspicion, credulity and intolerance, in which unity of feeling and belief is the sole requirement and all exercise of private judgment is condemned as treason, enables the journalist to exercise an almost boundless will to power. He sees the tide of popular emotions swell and flow to the stroke of his pen. He finds satisfaction in watching the gudgeon eagerly rising to the artful bait of his war-truth. As the removal of the upper layers of personal responsibility and customary restraints proceeded, and the naked herd-mind in all the simplicity of barbarism obtruded, the journalists of all countries became its avowed priests and prophets, finding each day the inspired ritual, the inflammatory liturgy and the victims for the sacrifice. For the chief symptom of the civilian war-mind was a sort of instinctive throwback to the superstitiousness of the savage horde, fear-stricken by some "hidden hand" and eager to avert the unknown wrath of an offended deity.

It was not, indeed, a definite state of mind. But the process of the war-hysteria was shot through with suggestions of this reversion to primitive horde-life. The witch-smelling, the heresy-hunts, the popular persecutions of all times, carry in them some obscure but terrible fear of "the accursed thing" and of the persons who harbour it, and the need of discovery and expiation. It may be that traces of the belief in human sacrifice wiping out sin lurk all the time in such outbreaks as we have witnessed. For this persecuting mania has by no means been directed exclusively against enemy aliens, reputed pro-Germans, or even conscientious objectors. It has assailed men and women of conspicuous loyalty, who had taken no known part in thwarting or in crossing popular sentiment. The method by which this resentment was aroused was some utterly unfounded and unsupported suggestion of hidden treason, of harbouring "the accursed thing." Any eccentricity of behaviour, any conduct that the neighbours could not understand, sufficed to breed a mythology of treason.

But when this temper assumed national dimensions, it was always the baser journalism that was its propagator. There seemed to gather in the general mind thick vapours of irrational suspicion capable of precipitation into any monstrous shape. It belonged to the Press to give direction by the conscious exercise of a malicious and unscrupulous invention. The episode of the Black Book, in which treason and nameless personal depravity were the common bond of a secret and infamous confederation comprising many of the most famous persons of the land, was the culminating achievement of this wave of superstition and credulity. A rally of the surviving powers of common sense after the exposure of this extraordinary matter dispersed for a while the vapours out of which these spectres grew. But the incident deserves close consideration by the social pathologist.

It has been admitted that these follies and the journalism which preys on them are not discoveries of war-time. Such irrational propensities of the herd-mind are always the quarry of artful publicists and politicians. But the war emergency aggravated them in two ways. The first, the repression of the exercise of private judgment as an unpatriotic obstacle to national unity, has already been observed. The other is the positive manufacture of a common mind by propaganda. The very title "propaganda" is a testimony to the irrationality of the process. It implies a wholesale planting of news or opinion on a contagious mind by a common method, in which there is little or no regard to the personal make-up of the recipient. Propaganda posits the herd-mind, suggestible, receptive, uncritical and unresisting. If the process were confined to the spreading of news, leaving the news to produce its effect upon the individual minds in accordance with their personal interests and valuations, it might be very serviceable. But it is not. In every nation such propaganda has been launched with the express intention of producing opinion and stimulating passion by the selection, rejection and presentation of news without any close regard to evidence or inherent probability. To secure a uniformity of opinion and to support the fighting spirit of the nation have been the related objects of this process. To this end every effective instrument has been utilized, pulpit, platform, "pictures," music-hall, but most of all the Press.

Never before has the power of collective and repeated suggestion been practised with so much conscious skill and success. The barriers of separate personality having been removed, the public mind presented a smooth plastic surface for the common impressions. Opinion and feeling could be fashioned and directed with ease and certainty by the liberation of news kept in governmental storage, and tricked out with provocative headlines and stimulating editorial comment. Thus came into circulation a Government war-truth which warped the minds of innocent men and women as insidiously as the war-finance picked their pockets. This unscrupulous behaviour was held to be necessitated by the sudden reversion to a primitive struggle for group-life. It was the Prussian doctrine of necessity, the Machiavellian "reason of state." Though the sharp issue was habitually evaded, the true meaning and defence of this propaganda, with its defiance of the rules of reason and of honesty, were that it was necessary to present an unbroken fighting front to the enemy. The mind of the fighting nation must be "doped" like the brain and stomach of the men in the front trench waiting to go over the top. The economy of truth, first employed to deceive the enemy, thus passed by what appeared a logical necessity into self-deceit.

The first stage in the process was concealment of facts relating to the plans and instruments of war which, if disclosed, might prove useful to the enemy. The difficulty of discriminating between useful and useless information of this kind led to an ever-tightening censorship upon all communication of war intelligence. But, as more and more of our industrial and other organized civilian activities became closely ancillary to war, the censorship extended to large branches of information relating to our engineering and chemical works, shipping and railways, and any other businesses affecting either the efficiency of our fighting forces or the material resources of our home population. Concealment from the enemy everywhere implied concealment from our own people. But our rulers and their Press soon recognized that information of an engineering strike or an explosion in a munition factory was not only useful to the enemy but damaging to the spirit of our people, and therefore to be concealed from them.

It was this acceptance of the duty of concealing facts likely to depress the spirit of the people which led us to the important advance from the negative interference with truth, called censorship, to the positive processes of propaganda. For, if it is injurious to "let down" or depress the popular spirit, it is advantageous to "buck it up." Our enemy had given a most audacious lead by disseminating useful news and moulding opinion not only in their own but in neutral countries. *Fas est et ab hoste doceri.* Fairly launched upon this novel and adventurous career, our Government and Press combined to boost our cause by operating upon public opinion. At first, we could represent this propaganda as essentially defensive, the countering of enemy propaganda. But, as in military operations, the partition between the defensive and offensive cannot be maintained. Large bodies of our intellectuals were mobilized for this work, and factories of war-truth soon produced a considerable output, while a distributive system of lecturers and colporteurs was spread over the country.

Controversy in the proper sense there was none. For law, public opinion and mob violence conspired to reduce to impotence all attempts of a recalcitrant or critical minority to question war-truths or to expose the methods of their manufacture. We speak of it as factory work, for the essential character of the process was the grinding out of graded packet goods for consumption and assimilation by millions of minds planed down to a common credulity and receptivity. Such art, or artfulness, as was displayed consisted in choosing the particular tap of stimulant or sedative to be turned on to meet some "peace offensive" or to cover up some awkward incident.

A foremost branch of this propaganda, the production and dissemination of war-atrocities, deserves some special notice here, because it bears a peculiar testimony to the mental degradation of war. The attribution of atrocities to the enemy is, of course, a familiar occurrence in all wars. Atrocities are always committed by invading armies, and even when they do not occur they are imputed and believed. History will doubtless affirm that the German invasion of Belgium and France was attended by a great deal of intentional and organized brutality calculated to gain certain military ends, in addition to the sporadic brutality which usually accompanies invasion. The record of such abominations naturally rouses the indignation of the suffering nation, its allies, and the neutral world against the perpetrators. But the deliberate and industrious hoarding of these stories of atrocity, their literary cultivation and systematic handling, in order to inflame hatred and feed war passion, are novel and peculiarly degrading features in the psychology of war. It is hard to say whether this demoralizes more the agents or the patients of such propaganda. For the facility with which men of high intellectual attainments and scrupulous judgment have been brought to stamp with their authority as proven facts statements made by passionate partisans under circumstances of national excitement, and admitting no such cross-examination as a judicial inquiry deems essential to the veracity of statements thus obtained, is the most striking of all testimonies to that submergence of higher personality which we have found to be the heaviest moral cost of war. The journalists and other middlemen of propaganda suffer less specific injury because they are by the ordinary practice of their craft accustomed to deal more lightly with evidence. But the direct co-operation and encouragement of the Government in the least reputable arts of treating news and moulding opinion has left journalism a more dangerous enemy to reason and humanity than ever before. For its power is perceptibly enhanced and its sense of responsibility diminished.

CHAPTER IV

THE SUBMERGENCE OF PERSONALITY

THE war-mind is best studied in the educated classes. There the surrender of what is most personal or individual in temper and disposition shows itself with most distinctness. Swept along by the "consciousness of kind," our intellectuals freely sacrificed their critical faculty upon the altar of patriotism, exulting in the comfort and security which they liked to regard as discipline. And, indeed, the fear-begotten huddling for warmth and safety, when the sacred barriers of class and standing were lowered to permit a generous sociality and a free co-operation for the common good, had its amiable aspect. The easy contacts between gentry and shopkeepers, employer and employed, rich and poor, seemed to some war-enthusiasts the beginning of the social millennium. For everybody to be told what to do and to be glad to do it appeared a remedy for all the troublesome intestinal diseases of Society. Soldiers were under discipline. In the new war, waged with all the resources of the nations, civilians, too, must be under discipline. So this condition of the herd-mind came to be called discipline.

But the submergence of personality is not really discipline. Even in the soldier it is not. For though an automatic and mechanically accurate response to the word of command belongs to military virtue, it by no means exhausts its meaning. In every grade of military service some personal initiative and responsibility survives as an essential of success: the individual will must be kept alive, if it be only for endurance. Nor does the soldier's relations either to his fellows or to his enemy cancel the personality so completely as in the civilian herd-mind. *Esprit de corps* is both tempered by and expressed in a comradeship which nourishes some fine qualities of personality. Moreover, it is especially noteworthy that the purely collective sentiments towards the enemy, as well as the intensity of hate, are far less marked among the combatants than among the spectators.[1] "Jingoism" is a spectatorial passion. It is natural that this should be so. For the soldier acquires some realization of the enemy as consisting of human beings more or less like himself in their personal ways of going on, and subject to the same conditions. The mind of the civilian spectator, on the other hand, having less vent for his sharpened feelings in directly relevant activities, and watching from a distance the great aggregate of movements and events, loses all sense of the personal factors that are involved, except so far as the few relatives and friends he has at the front are concerned. As he watches with a fearful fascination the play of impersonal forces, over which he is conscious of exercising no control, his civilian discipline becomes a superstitious servility. He is the tribesman cowering before the authority of his chief and the fetishes and taboos of the tribe: the images of King and Country, the

[1] Cf. Philip Gibbs, *Realities of War*, *passim*.

portrait of Kitchener, the stabbing words of placards, the dictates of Controllers, become "the word of the Lord," to question which is the unpardonable sin.

It is sometimes contended that this temporary abandonment of liberty and personality is a sound policy for such an emergency as war. War revives the primitive needs of the biological struggle for survival. Individual or factional criticism and the exercise of personal choice and judgment are so much friction on the wheels of the war chariot. The personal rights good for peace are bad for war. By this argument have been defended military and industrial conscription, the persecution of conscientious objectors, the repression of liberties of speech, Press and meeting, the imprisonment upon suspicion and without trial by administrative action, and, in short, the claim of absolute power by the Executive. The accepted maxim, *inter arma silent leges*, includes the abrogation of all personal rights and the substitution of the sovereign will of the State. It is admitted that this doctrine and practice are pure Prussianism, that they are intolerable in time of peace, but it is held that they are necessary for the duration of the war. It is unsafe to dogmatize upon what is a very delicate and difficult problem of social economy. "In a tight place you must do anything to win," or, in other words, necessity knows no law. Such is the contention. Such was the defence which German statecraft gave for invading Belgium. We say a false defence, because there was no such "necessity." That may very well be true. But once grant this plea of necessity and you soon discover that necessity is a matter of degree and is stretched to cover every strong case of utility.

An excellent instance was the Secret Treaty under which we undertook to deliver to Italy lands and populations to which she had no rightful claim, and which were not ours to give. The importance of getting Italy into the war and evoking her best effort presented itself in the guise of a "necessity," and on that ground alone has our assent to this treaty been defended. But only in a constructive or secondary sense can the term "necessity" be applied here: it was necessary only to improve our chance of success in the grand struggle. The syllogism runs thus: It is necessary for us to win: this action assists us to win: therefore this action is necessary. But in the first place, the minor premise is in its form defective. Everything that helps is not essential to success. Even the truth of the major premise may be questioned. In what sense is it *necessary* to win? It is, we argue, a moral necessity, in the sense that the right is on our side and that it is morally necessary for the right to triumph. But granting the right is on our side, may every sort of wrong be committed in defending "the right"? May we give Italy the property of another in order to punish Germany for wronging Belgium? Along this declivity one soon reaches the lower moral level of "All is fair in love and war," a concise, popular application of this doctrine of necessity to the two chief fields of the biological struggle.

Indeed, so far as war goes, experience shows that this maxim is closely operative. There is nothing an enemy may not be driven to do in an extremity, no act of cruelty or treachery against his opponent, no invasion of the rights of neutrals. Thus necessity is at last reduced to the convenience of the moment. True, we are apt to defend each inhuman practice by alleging the example of the enemy. But this is a weakness in the logic of war. For, if we are justified in using poison gas or in bombing undefended towns, in order not to leave to the enemy whatever advantage accrues from these barbarities, we are justified in initiating these or any other practices, on the ground that they conduce to our success and shorten the destruction of war. "He did it first" confesses shame without avoiding guilt: the charge recoils on the confessor.

There will be some (they are called moralists) who will plead in ancient style that, as there are certain deeds which the virtuous man should rather die than do, so there are likewise deeds so essentially degrading to a nation that its statesmen or its generals should not sanction them, however "necessary" they may seem. Better our nation perish than win salvation by such dishonour!

But here, perhaps, we have wandered into a moral impasse. For even a sin-stained life of freedom may seem preferable to destruction or (the real issue) to subjection to a still more guilty enemy. Let us, therefore, return to the more profitable inquiry whether the repression of liberty and personality in war-time, in order to present a smooth unbroken front to the enemy, is a true policy in civilized society. Is this servile, credulous, passionate, vainglorious, uncritical herd-mind necessary or serviceable for "survival" purposes? Granted that it is sound tactics for buffaloes or wolves, or for primitive men, is it sound for a civilized community? Can reason, private judgment, personal control, contribute so little to the conduct of a modern nation in jeopardy of its life that they are rightly jettisoned in order to throw ourselves upon the self-protective instincts evolved for protection against the dangers that beset our ancestors in neolithic times? Can it be pretended that these blind emotional defences afford the best available security against the intricate designs of modern aggression? No one pretends it of military defence. That is a science and an art, and demands for its practitioners, or at least for many of them, the retention and application of high qualities of personality. But can the true economy for civilian defence be essentially different? Will a good buffalo-mind, consolidated into instinctive unity, do what is wanted?

No. Personal qualities of judgment, reason, imagination, initiative, self-control, are evidently endowed with high survival value, both for the individual and for society. They are evolved for this end, and the more critical the emergency the greater their value. Nor will it suffice to say that the national discipline of war-time confines the exercise of these high personal qualities to the leaders, and demands of the followers a blind obedience. It is not true that such absolute authority is good for a nation at war. Certain emergency powers are rightly exercised by the executive government under these circumstances and certain limitations of individual liberty follow. Espionage and other communication with the enemy, enemy trading, must be stopped, and this stoppage involves censorship of news and other regulations and restrictions. Movement of troops and supplies of war materials must have priority in transport and in other economic arrangements, involving various curtailments of ordinary private facilities. Such restraints upon liberty of action are the necessary backstrokes of war.

But there are two rightful conditions for the exercise of these emergency powers. The first is that the powers claimed should be definite in scope and application; the second, a corollary, is that persons arrested under these emergency laws should be charged and tried in accordance with the established usages of justice in their country. The violation of these elementary principles of British law and justice under the administration of D.O.R.A. did not help to win the war. The arrest and imprisonment of many persons without charge or trial, the prosecution and punishment of others for uttering words or circulating literature alleged but not proved to interfere with recruiting or to undermine military discipline, or for being in possession of such literature, or for other infractions of the elastic orders of "the competent military authority," so far from helping to "defend the realm," undermined the moral securities upon which the realm is built.

It has been contended that these arbitrary acts were necessary in order to cope with active treason. But our law had ample provisions for the trial and punishment of persons charged with this crime. It was not active treason against which these arbitrary powers were directed, but freedom of speech and publication of opinion. Now, the attempt to stop or stifle liberty of opinion is the most fatal act a Government can commit. For it saps the moral confidence of the people upon whose will or consent the Government professes to be based. A reasonable and informed public opinion is particularly necessary to support that larger practical authority claimed by a State at war. The right of free criticism of public policy and of access to all knowledge needed to make such criticism effective which can safely be communicated is the prime guaranty of public sanity. No Government can be released from the wholesome check of this free criticism. The attempt of a Government not merely to stop the free formation and expression of opinion, but to fashion an authorized and uniform opinion by subsidized propaganda is the deadliest of all attacks on liberty.

For if the will and consent of the people can be doped and moulded according to the desire and interest of the persons who compose the Government, the representative system is reduced to an empty form, devoid of intellectual or moral content. And it cannot be denied that this doping and moulding of opinion was practised. Nor was it merely a war measure. Long after the war was over it has been continued. The peace-making at Paris and the important happenings over half the Continent during that time and since have been subjected to Governmental selection, suppression and falsification, in order that public opinion may not work freely.

This deliberate suppression of the vital activities of a free personality during the war in order to produce and maintain an unintelligent and unreasoning unanimity was a damaging economy in war-time. For a Government endowed with absolute power and released from criticism plunged into follies and extravagances which brought us several times to the very brink of military disaster, leaving a legacy of political and financial perils for peace statecraft to grapple with. But these evils of military autocracy are not the worst results. The suppression of free personality has left moral scars, the serious nature of which we only realize when the restoration of normal conditions of life and work demand a return of the reasonable mind. After five years' submergence, how can it be expected that a people should at once recover the qualities of clear judgment and self-restraint, consideration and fair play, they are now called upon to exercise in the processes of social reconstruction? Time is wanted for recovery. It is a race with time. Unless recovery can set in fast enough, the civilization of Europe is passing into dissolution. How deeply has the poison of war entered into the mind of the peoples, how quickly may it pass away? Can we yet say with Prospero?—

> The charm dissolves apace;
> And as the morning steals upon the night,
> Melting the darkness, so their rising senses
> Begin to chase the ignorant fumes that mantle
> Their clearer reason. . . .
> Their understanding
> Begins to swell, and the approaching tide
> Will shortly fill the reasonable shores
> That now lie foul and muddy.

PART III

THE TRAGI-COMEDY OF WAR-IDEALISM

CHAPTER I

IDEALISM OF THE POLITICIANS

Tout comprendre c'est tout pardonner does not go far enough. For pardon retains an emotional content which would seem to disappear before complete understanding. Such understanding would bring moral indifference—neither praise nor blame, love nor hate.

It often seems as if the science of Human Nature made for this goal. A familiarization with the hidden motives of man, though it would not make us indifferent to the effects of conduct, would weaken the emotional valuations which rest upon imputing the responsibility for good and bad acts to the performers.

That is why the natural man, who wants to love and hate, distrusts and fears the scientific explanations which threaten to rob him of his cherished emotional reactions.

The resentment against Darwinian biology, and the geology which was its early premonitor and support, lay not so much in the degradation of man, by placing him in the animal kingdom, as in the sort of instinctive repugnance against any explanations which would impede the free flow of praise and blame. The interest of life appeared to depend upon the maintenance of accepted moral values. If man were animalized and brought under " the reign of law " these values would evaporate.

To stop this desecration troops of intellectual smoothers were called in to reconcile science and conventional morality, by reinstating the spiritual quality of life and restoring the delicate poise of a personal free-will. But no sooner was the task done to the popular satisfaction than fresh invasions upon our emotional liberties were made under the guise of psychology and sociology. To analyse, collect and measure the operations of the mind or soul, in individuals or in groups, is felt to be a disturbing and a perilous study. For some time it was sought to ward it off, or to belittle it, by representing it as pseudo-science, too slippery in material and too inexact in method to deserve intellectual attention or to yield reliable results. But as soon as psychology had escaped from the early *a priori* formulas which sought to bind it, and began its free experimental researches into the secret history of man, the intrinsic interests of the study enabled it to overcome the scientific boycott. And when it penetrated the ethics, politics and economics of social institutions, and began to shed new light upon the operations of group-life in tribes and nations, the commanding importance of the new social criticism it opened up made it the centre of a spiritual struggle as fierce as that which for so many centuries had waged round the now dismantled battlements of orthodox theology.

Indeed, it is clear that the struggle of the established social order against the new psychology is in essence a continuation of the struggle of theology against the science of the mid-nineteenth century. The same passions are involved and many of the same strategic positions are occupied. The charges of materialism and of destructive determinism brought against the Darwinians are now brought against the psycho-analysts and the scientific socialists. Nor is this a mere coincidence, if, as the new social criticism contends, theology has its chief significance as a defensive outpost of a statical society.

It can, therefore, be no matter of surprise that in our schools to-day Patriotism is displacing the older Piety, with its bible of imperial history, its ritual worship of the flag, its commemorative saints'-days, its drill-processionals and its consecrated vestments. The mystical sentiments which formerly were directed towards a distant deity are now claimed for the State and the social-economic order it seeks to ensure—and this not now in Germany, but in England and America.

What is the meaning of this consecration of the secular? We are told it is for the nourishment of ideals in the young and for the spiritual discipline demanded for good citizenship. And it is right that full recognition should be given to the sincerity of this conviction. The fear lest selfish materialism and class violence should destroy our civilization, and the belief that they can best be continued by cultivating national idealism, are very natural.

It is precisely in the comedy of this idealism, and of the genuine passion which it carries, that our new psycho-physics and its attendant sociology find their richest material, and it is in the criticism of this idealism that its fascination resides.

For what is the relation of tragedy and comedy towards ideals? Tragedy is the dramatic revelation of some higher unsuspected power, the unconquerable will of man triumphant over suffering and death itself, a sacrifice for some cause dearer than life itself, or the dramatic manifestation of some higher will than man's, vindicating a moral order in the world. The purging or purification of the emotions, of which Aristotle wrote, is an imperfect description of an art or act whose direct achievement is the epiphany of a spiritual ideal. Sin, suffering, insight, such is the order of the tragedy.

And what then of comedy? Its essence is a pleasing disillusionment, the exposure of sham ideals. Low comedy indeed moves along the surface of life, creating and resolving false situations and exhibiting quaint conceits of manner and behaviour, pricking the lighter bubbles of make-believe. But true comedy dips deep into the well of life. Its material is the revelation of the hidden design in the texture of life, the contrast between the conscious and the unconscious motives of conduct. The conscious deceit of hypocrisy is not comic in itself; the comedy lies in the false ideal in the mind of those who are "taken in" and in the spectatorial expectation of the discovery. But hypocrisy is no fine food for the comic spirit. For it belongs to that spirit, as Meredith has pointed out, to range freely over the whole of life, lightly lifting the veil of illusion which is everywhere woven round us and our doings. This spirit is no harsh moralist, no cynic, but a genial showman exhibiting the freakishness of a human nature which we imagine has been got under control and the strange dances it leads us all. This criticism of life is essentially the work of the creative and interpretative imagination. But this art, like every other, feeds on science, or ordered and tested knowledge. And so psychology and sociology, instead of killing comedy by reducing life to law, continually open up new vistas of hazard and surprise. If human nature were the simple box of properties and faculties it once seemed to be, science might rob life of its charm by dissolving its mystery. But such science as we have, or can have, will not stale the infinite variety of psychic life.

. . . . .

To approach the Great War, its origins and issues, from the standpoint of Comedy will be taken as a blasphemy by those who resent scrutiny into their "ideals." Its horrors and its sufferings should render it immune against such levity! This sentiment, indeed, is one of those irrational defences which always impede wholesome inquiry into human values. This man, this institution, this doctrine is so sacrosanct that such inquiry is impertinence. But how if Comedy be the finest of Socratic methods, the divine irony by which the truth of every claim to sanctity is tested, the best way of ascertaining what a man, or mankind, is really after—in short, the discovery of his soul?

If Comedy is not the only art of this discovery, it is surely one, and none the less useful because it works by revelation and surprise. And it is supremely interested in declared ideals, the high motives by which men and peoples on great occasions and in great doings believe themselves and others to be inspired. Now, it is acknowledged to be a sign of spiritual grace that no modern war can be presented to any civilized people that engages in it in any other than "ideal" terms. For freedom, justice and humanity every modern war is fought, and by both sides. Such idealization of war-origins is a commonplace of history. The nature of its sincerity is matter for interesting reflection. But in one respect this war appears to most of its idealists to differ from all previous wars. The ideals of other wars were tarnished by their origin and conduct and falsified by their results. But not this war. We have the testimony of *The Times* to the effect that "The war proved for ever that idealism in action is the master-force in modern politics."[1] The comic spirit surely pricks up its ears when it hears these words and swiftly rehearses the record of this ponderous prophet of idealism.

In ordinary politics *The Times* would be the last quarter in which to look for the championship of ideals. Such a declaration may, therefore, be taken as a register of the high-water mark of the flood of idealism which the British war-spirit evoked. Idealism must in such a case be taken to mean emotion directed to the achievement of ideals, and if we are to understand this "master-force" we must consider how the mind of a normally cold and practical people became seized by this moral feeling for ideals. But just a word about the relation of "ideals" towards "ideas." In ordinary times, it is not too much to say that an "ideal" is, not merely for *The Times*, but for its readers and for our people in general, a term of disparagement. It is a vague presentation of an "idea," which is itself distinguished from what is "real." Ideals are blurred visions of things which, if not quite unreal, are unattainable, and idealists are in this disparaging sense visionaries.

Now why has war come to reverse this estimate

[1] *The Times*, editorial, September 22, 1919.

and to give a supreme value to what for ordinary man and woman are valueless? Is not this reversal, in the first place, an unconscious or half-conscious testimony to the reality and force of a mental and moral attitude commonly conceived as both foolish and dangerous? For the general conviction of the unsubstantiality of ideals for ordinary conduct of affairs carries with it a reprobation of idealists as dangerous persons possessed by a vision which, though false, is somehow capable of generating great effort and self-sacrifice. Hence, at a time when there is great need for effort and self-sacrifice, one must have recourse to political idealism, just as one does to that particular form of idealism called religion for spiritual consolation in moments of personal sorrow. Idealism in politics, and particularly in war, the most critical act of politics, is *imprimis* an emotional boost. This must not, however, be taken to imply that the ideals to which the emotion is directed are false or that the emotion is insincere. For it may well be that in great national or personal emergencies certain reserve funds of emotion, normally unrecognized or neglected, may be drawn upon. This, I take it, is actually the case with these herd-feelings of war-passion which, defensive or offensive, express themselves in the decorative forms and colours which we call ideals. The amalgam of group-affection, fear, suspicion, self-esteem, hate, which comprises the war-passion, weaves for itself banners of the ideal under which to march with greater verve and solidarity to victory. There is real stuff in this emotion of the ideal which leads men to fight for their country. But this real stuff dresses itself up in formulas and images which are curiously remote from the emotional realities of the members of the herd. That is why "idealism in action" plays such strange pranks with the ideals.

When the statesmen at the opening of the war unfurled the banner on which were inscribed freedom, the public law of Europe and the rights of small nationalities, are we to picture them with tongue in cheek because they may have been aware of other less disinterested motives which underlay our war-policy? When they formally disclaimed all thoughts of territorial or other gains,[1] must the fruits of victory which, as we say, "fell to us" be adduced as proof of their insincerity in these disclaimers?

The deeper comedy of life lies in the nature of sincerity. "It is but a shallow haste which concludeth insincerity from what outsiders call inconsistency—putting a dull mechanism of 'ifs' and 'therefores' for the living myriad of hidden suckers whereby the belief and the conduct are wrought into mutual sustainment."

If we start with the assumption that sincerity is a question of manner and degree, we shall not do wrong. Popular cynicism appraises far too low the

[1] Mr. Asquith, Cardiff, October 2, 1914:
"We have no desire to add to our Imperial burdens either in area or responsibility."
Mr. Bonar Law, House of Commons, December 22, 1916:
"We are not fighting for territory, we are not fighting for the greater strength of those who are fighting."
Mr. Lloyd George, *New York Times*, February 12, 1917:
"We are not fighting a war of conquest."
Mr. Long, House of Commons, February 20, 1917:
"It all depends upon whether you are determined . . . to secure such a victory as will give us, not aggrandisement of territory, not any extension of our Empire, but will give us the right to ask for ourselves along with our Allies for such a peace and a conclusion as will make the repetition of this war impossible."

sincerity of most great politicians. It may almost be said that the politician is accorded a licence to be insincere, and that his hearers even acquire a customary discount of his values. But such cynicism certainly overshoots the mark. Just as the clearly conscious hypocrite in private life is almost always a mythical monster, so the picture of the astute calculating politician, consciously playing on the foibles of the people by simulating convictions and sentiments which he knows he does not really hold, is equally a counterfeit presentment. What does happen to the politician, in moments of high interest or great emergency, is something quite different from this cold calculation. The successful politician is generally a man whose natural aptitude for seeing in a favourable light any cause, party, or line of conduct to which he is attached transcends the ordinary. His imaginative sympathy puts a glow of enthusiasm into every policy in which he embarks, brushes aside all selfish or sordid aims that may adhere to it, and presents it in the best light it is capable of taking. When Mr. Lloyd George, fastening upon the outrages to Belgium and to Serbia at the opening of war, appealed to the defence of rights of small nationalities as the ideal motive of the war, was he insincere because he placed in the background the larger and the less emotional aspects of war-policy? No. On his feet and facing his audience, Mr. Lloyd George in heart and imagination was filled to the exclusion of all else with the bully and his victim, and with the sentiment of the little nationality as typified by Belgium. It was this genuine feeling and the dramatic art of communicating it to others that led him thus to simplify and to idealize the situation.

Or take another type of political sincerity, given in the famous appeal of Mr. Asquith for the substitution of justice for contending armaments and "a precarious equipoise of power." Here was a flash of deeper insight into an ideal purpose of the war with less immediate emotional appeal than the other. Doubtless the intellectual faith of a trained lawyer, kindled to enthusiasm by an apprehension of the terrible urge of events, lifted Mr. Asquith to this height of prophetic utterance.

This to him was for the moment the real meaning of the war, its ideal purpose to which he gave such felicitous expression. No one would contend that Mr. Asquith had brought any deep continuous volume of constructive energy towards even the initiation of this better Europe, or had rendered the least assistance to the little band of internationalists who had sought to lay the foundations of pacific order.

Again, no one knew better the reality and strength of the unideal aims and motives which underlay the tangled pre-war policy of all the European Governments. It was, therefore, an emotionally thin form of sincerity which underlay the dramatization of war-purpose given by Mr. Asquith.

But these statesmen and their friends rightly resent charges of conscious insincerity based upon comparisons of professed ideals and their realization in the fruits of victory.

CHAPTER II

IDEALISM OF THE PEOPLES

BUT now, turning from the somewhat ignominious spectacle of the idealism of politicians, let us examine the wide tragi-comedy of popular idealism in the war. Both sides proclaimed it a War of Ideals. Germany fought for the defence of the Fatherland and for the extension of German Kultur in a great civilizing mission. The Allies fought for Freedom, Justice and Democracy against the tyranny of Prussian military autocracy and the political and economic domination it designed to fasten on the world. Each side conceived its own ideals to be the sole inspiring and directive motive of its policy, and the idealization of the enemy to be sheer hypocrisy. Though a few German military leaders may have taken a purely realistic view of the meaning of the war as an instrument of power, the German people had been subjected to a long education in the mission of German Kultur, with force as a wedge to open opportunities. With them war had a recognized place in the accepted scheme of idealism.

The British idealization was a more sudden and more naïve performance. For though Britain had long played so large a practical part in "world politics," it cannot be held that this word or the idea it connotes ever entered the conscious mind of the great majority even of our educated classes. A few busybodies had engaged themselves in recent years in an attempt to put popular thought and feeling behind the mission of British Imperialism. But the popular mind was virgin soil for political idealism when the war broke out.

Yet even this statement needs qualification. For a rude but serviceable idealization of a semi-conscious order must be held to belong to the image of "John Bull" which the English nation has presented to itself and to the world as typical of our character and interests.

Indeed, the cleverest thing we have done, in our collective capacity, is to foist upon the world as our authentic portrait this jovial simpleton, a stupid, overfed, honest, plain-spoken fellow, contented with his lot, and to all appearances a fairly obvious prey for his keener-witted and less scrupulous neighbours. Suspicious persons who express surprise at his immense and continuous success in worldly matters are usually told of the series of undesigned events which have worked out the curious pattern of his greatness. According to one of his authoritative exponents, he built his world-wide Empire in "a fit of absence of mind." In fact, whenever he sets about anything, he carefully abstains from thinking out his course. He trusts to Providence, "carries on," and somehow "muddles through." But, thanks to the same Providence, he never comes out empty-handed. Though he never went in "for the goods," he finds them in his portmanteau when he comes out, and he cannot explain how they got there.

Take the Great War for an example. No selfish,

sordid motive stained the purity of his intentions as a belligerent. He responded to the call of duty and the appeal of high ideals. Slow to anger, reluctant to take up arms, our peaceful people, fearless on their own account, with nothing to gain and all to lose save honour and self-respect, threw in their lot with Belgium, France and Serbia for the defence of public law, the rights of small nations and the sanctity of treaty obligations against the criminal aggression of the Central Powers.

It is true that in our casual way we had been making what might be called preparations against this eventuality for some time past, by diplomatic arrangements with France and Russia, which, containing no formal or admitted obligations, proved to have the binding force of treaties, and that we had surveyed the continental field quite carefully with a view to the disposition of our expeditionary force and our Navy. But such considerations do not modify our clear conviction that we were caught unprepared and dragged into the great conflict for purely disinterested reasons. This attitude we preserved throughout the struggle, and we issued from this "peace of right and justice" with the same conscious rectitude. We fought to save Belgium and France, to restore Alsace-Lorraine, to win liberty for the Poles, the Jugo-Slavs and Czecho-Slovaks, to break the foul tyranny of the Turks and to make it impossible for Prussian militarism to dominate the world.

But there are ill-conditioned cavillers in foreign countries, and even among our own people, who insist that we have not "served God for naught." They point to certain incidental and wholly unintended gains, which come to us from the rearrangement of the world, and call them spoils of war. They allude to our pre-war fears and jealousy of German trade, and the complete extirpation of that trade from all parts of the world achieved by the peace; the destruction of German shipping and finance, which leaves an uncontested field for British enterprise. The British Navy has now an undisputed mastery of the seas, with an incomparable provision of coaling and wireless stations. The mandatory principle, which our representatives imposed upon the Covenant of the League, is to bring another two million square miles of territory within the British Empire, including the rich untapped resources of Mesopotamia. Egypt passed silently under the veil of war into our Protectorship. Virtually, the whole of the German Colonies come to us and our Dominions. Upon the League of Nations, the future instrument of world government, the British Empire is to have six voices to one of each of the other Powers in the assembly.

Yet, issuing with this enormous access of territory, power and commercial opportunity, we do not recognize that these gains qualify or discredit in the least degree the lofty disinterestedness of our professions. We are even pained and indignant that other people, who do things with definite intentions, impute the same to us, and when we deny them apply the rude word "hypocrisy." We resent this crude and shallow diagnosis of Bull's "idealism." We are even justified in feeling this resentment. For the moral glow of indignation at the wickedness of his enemy, and the enthusiasm for liberty and justice with which Bull has always girded on his armour against tyrants and aggressors —Napoleon, Nicholas or William—cannot be dismissed as conscious make-believe or as mere spiritual dope. It is a moral necessity of his nature that he should appear to himself as a crusader when the hidden stress of circumstances impels him to fight. That stress, no doubt, is largely compacted of the secret passions and interests which in the end take concrete shape in more territory and power and the good things of this earth. But these things must not figure in his consciousness as motives, and they do not; hence the genuineness of his indignation when he is confronted with the goods in his possession and charged with going after them.

There is a fine spiritual artistry in this, which envious outsiders will call artfulness. Bull's inner self—his conscience, shall we say?—somehow makes him aware that, if he went straight and open-eyed for his selfish interests, he would fail. His march must be a mission, his aims must be ideals. So he keeps a better self to dress these ideals for him when they are wanted.

We are not, perhaps, in a position to understand, and therefore to forgive, the failure of the Allies to translate the idealism of the war into terms of peace and settlement. The failure was so open and complete as to rejoice the heart of the cynic. Idealism was just what he had always held it to be, "fine words" that do "butter parsnips," creating an atmosphere of spiritual uplift which helps practical men to put things through. Never was there a finer and a more economical display of such idealism than in the parade of principles in this war "to make the world safe for democracy."

This idealism was twice blest. It helped to boost our own war efforts and to undermine those of the enemy. For the crowning triumph of our idealism was that it imposed itself upon the enemy. This, perhaps, was the great contribution of America towards the war-idealism. So drilled had Germans been in the lesson of "British hypocrisy" that it was difficult for the fine language of Mr. Lloyd George about having no quarrel with the German people, or his promises of a fair future to a democratic Germany, to make much way. But when the high-priest of democracy himself blew upon the horn, chanted the holy words and the Allied statesmen and peoples solemnly repeated "Amen!" the romantic German mind was overreached. When the idealism of the Fourteen Points and the Five Principles was formally presented to the German people as the basis of peace, in return for full surrender and the overthrow of the Hohenzollern government, the Germans actually believed that America would keep her word and prevent the less scrupulous Allies from "bolting" their idealism. In this faith they made their revolution and laid down their arms. The conduct of the Allies and Associated Powers at Paris falsified this faith. Idealism had done its work and was put upon the shelf: the real politics of Clemenceau and Pichon took its place.

Will sober historians pronounce this to be the record in the annals of public perfidy? So it doubtless seems to most Germans, and to some Britons and Americans, making a hasty comparison of profession and practice.

But our study of war-psychology may soften, if it cannot efface, this judgment. The Allied statesmen did not deliberately set this spiritual trap to catch the enemy. The fine air of enthusiasm with which the Allied nations welcomed Mr. Wilson's beautiful words was not sheer make-believe. There was some real recognition of the truth and moral value of these high professions. But except in a few quarters, that recognition was feeble and obscure. The popular reaction to any general principles is weaker than it seems. For vague enthusiasm can never compensate for lack of clear appreciation. And the mental grasp even of the more educated minds upon such terms as Self-Determination, nationality, equality of opportunity, is found to be exceedingly defective. The meaning which they had for ordinary citizens was one of extreme attenuation. They were "good words" and their acceptance and repetition made you "feel good." They were spiritual boost, and as such helped to win the war. And here the sincerity of the popular adoption got entangled with the art of propaganda, and it was that entanglement which more than anything else served to sap the sincerity of the ideals. For, as we have seen, the sort of war-truth made for propaganda was directed in its manufacture more by consideration of the credulity of the consumer than by any objective standard of veracity.

This helps us to understand how the passions of fear, greed, hate and revenge pushed aside the "idealism" of the Allies and stamped their impress on the terms of peace, without the peoples realizing their betrayal. Upon the great majority the ideals had never had more than a sentimental hold. Their incorporation in documents addressed to the enemy or to neutrals were displays of rhetorical highmindedness, not to be taken as pledges or obligations. Indeed, the number of persons in Britain and America is very small who are even aware that Mr. Wilson's Fourteen Points and his principles were definitely offered to Germany as the basis of peace. For the cunning of avoiding facts likely to prove inconvenient or damaging to one's dominant desires is subtle and widespread. We scent the danger from afar. If the inconvenient truth were actually thrust under our eyes, we might be too honest to ignore or deny it. So we keep it from coming near us by the manifold devices of a protective instinct which lets us know that certain persons, certain opinions, certain facts, are likely to cause us trouble. We take care not to be at home when they tap at our door. Had our war-idealism had a high degree of sincerity it would no doubt have made such an escape impossible. But its shallowness and feebleness easily allowed it to be thus outwitted. So the Allied peoples have never admitted even to themselves that their statesmen bought the surrender of the German arms by an undertaking to observe the "principles" of Mr. Wilson and to accord more favourable terms to a constitutional democracy than those they would impose on beaten Kaiserism.

But the comedy of idealism none the less permits them to plume themselves upon the application to the settlement of those very principles which they disclaimed as actual obligations. The general sentiment of the Allied peoples at the moment of the armistice was one of self-gratulation at their generosity in refraining from inflicting on the civilians of the Central Powers atrocities equivalent to those which the armies of these Powers had inflicted upon their civilians. This sentiment of Christian magnanimity was somehow compatible with a simultaneous feeling of exasperation at the thwarted passions for revenge, cloaked of course as "righteous retribution" and conceived as the only way of bringing home to the German people the consciousness of sin.

This emotion of feeling good because they had let Germany off easy, accompanied by a conviction that, whatever was the punishment inflicted in the terms of settlement, it must fall short of the merits of the case and so err on the side of mercy, made it unnecessary to scrutinize the Peace Treaties in order to discover whether they were in fact conformable to the ideals of freedom, justice and democracy for which the war had been fought. They saw that they liberated and restored France, Belgium and Serbia, that they freed Poland and the subject nationalities of Austro-Hungary and Turkey, and that the foundation of a League of Nations was laid which should prevent the occurrence of another world-war. This large loose view ignored the manufacture of new subject nationalities in France, Poland, Italy, Bohemia and Roumania, the open violation of the right of self-determination for Austria, the repudiation of all equality of economic opportunities for the conquered countries, the parcelling out of their colonies, foreign property and markets as loot among the victors, the conversion of the Council of the Big Three at Paris into the pretence of a League of Nations which would deal out justice to all peoples great and small and would administer the backward countries upon principles of the common welfare of mankind! Even the culminating impudence of the Big Three in announcing the division of the Mandated Areas among themselves without waiting for the operation of the League, which alone could give this act validity, aroused but a passing surprise.

It was no wonder that the general public should

feel satisfied that the "idealism" of the war was substantially realized in the settlements, when there were found among the statesmen directly responsible for the Peace those who asserted and defended this position. Not all of them would go so far as to declare with *The Times* that "This war has proved for ever that idealism is the master force in modern politics," or with Mr. Wilson in asserting that the Treaty contained nothing incompatible with his principles. But they contended that the compromises and qualifications of principle were small blemishes that did not seriously impair the justice and humanity of the Peace. After all, the amount of newly stolen territory and newly subjected populations was small in comparison with the quantity of liberation that had been effected. Just so might we commend the noble character of one who scrupulously kept all the commandments with only an occasional infraction of the sixth, the seventh and the eighth.

Then on the top of this defence is put the other, viz. that Mr Wilson and the idealists were beaten down by the realists, and forced to take such a mutilated version of their principles as the conditions of the diplomatic conflict enabled them to get. The hopeless inconsistency of these two defences does not prevent their emergence in close juxtaposition, an interesting commentary upon the chaotic thinking of our broken idealists.

Though this analysis of conscious motive acquits our responsible statesmen of the cruder charge of deliberate perfidy, it does not exonerate them from a grave charge which all the war-idealists must share in different degrees.

Their betrayal of ideals is due largely to the failure to give clear form to these ideals in the first place, and then to the failure to observe the facts of the peace in the light of their ideals. But this failure to make a clear presentation to themselves both of the ideals and of the facts is itself a moral defect. It is a blend of cowardice and cunning. Ideals, as we saw, were recognized for their value as spiritual boost. But, at the same time, there was a feeling that, if they were to seek to get translated from the spiritual realm into the practical world, they would be terribly obstructive to other less idealistic cravings which demanded satisfaction. There was a place for ideals, but not in the close neighbourhood of practical affairs !

If anybody questions and points to the achievement of certain war-aims, such as the liberation of Poland, the break-up of the Austrian Empire, the establishment of a League of Nations, as fruits of idealism, there is a simple test. If Poland is liberated by virtue of the ideal of self-determination, why not Ireland and India ? If subject nationalities are in conflict with the ideal in the enemy Empires, why not in the victorious Empires ? For the quality of a principle, an ideal, is that it is no respecter of particular parties or circumstances. If Ireland is held in bondage while Poland is released, the release of the latter is quite manifestly due not to the recognition of an ideal, a principle of nationality, but to a desire to punish and weaken our enemies. If a League of Nations is set up on a basis of partiality and inequality, designed to maintain in the world the supremacy of the Allies and to execute their will, it is idle to claim for it the virtue of true internationalism. A feeble and wandering idealism is always caught up and tripped by the keener, quicker selfish desires of men. But it is the fault of the idealist that it is weak and wandering. He keeps it so.

In discussing the self-imputed character of John Bull we caught a glimpse of the nature of our problem, the half-conscious conviction that it was better not to try to realize or rationalize our "ideal" and our "mission," but to keep them in a safe atmosphere of moral abstractions. For this enabled the Briton to get the best of both worlds. Even this refusal clearly to present to ourselves our ideals is not a deliberate policy but an almost entirely unconscious protective cunning, not a conviction but a feeling that security and success are thus attained. This enables us to resent with indignation the vulgar accusation of hypocrisy. Hypocrites we are not, but our sincerity is so heavily diluted that it ill-deserves the name. So heavily is the honey loaded with the wax which we use for deafening our ears to the higher voices.

But a still more remarkable instance of the method of the perversion of ideals is afforded by the Russian episode. The Allied invasion of a people with whom they were not properly "at war," the support by arms and money of every agent of reaction in that country, the massacre of countless innocents by a strangling blockade which is hardly sanctioned by international law in the case of ordinary belligerents, all this was represented by the Allied peoples to themselves as part of the struggle for democracy, a liberation of the Russian people from a criminal conspiracy of proletarian oppressors. How was this done? The answer is that the powers of greed, hate and fear became "a lying spirit in the mouth of the Lord's prophets." Their conduct was actuated by a deep concern for the ideals of freedom and genuine democracy in Russia! These ideals had been threatened by the poison of Bolshevism, injected by Germany, in its own war interests, to weaken Russia and make it a ready prey to the political and economic penetration of Germany. When Germany was broken and Bolshevism had overspread the whole of Russia, the continued intervention was defended by the reversal of the earlier plea. It was then necessary to break Bolshevism and restore a genuine and safe democracy, in order to prevent the poison flowing back again to Central Europe. What harm the noxious propaganda would have done to Germany if it had been permitted to return to the country of its origin does not appear.

Here is a curious sidelight upon the nature of war-idealism, that it renounces faith in the survival value of truth in the conflict of ideas, and believes that forcible suppression is the only safe way of handling false ideas.

Forcible action—the essence of war—displaces reason as the test and guarantee of truth. As justice is the right of the stronger, so truth becomes the opinion of the stronger. Falsehood, i.e. the opinion of the weaker, must be repressed as a breach in the intellectual and moral solidarity of the nation. The utterance of these unpopular opinions is disloyalty!

The conviction that forcible suppression of criticism and of competing ideals is a serviceable method of conserving and promoting the soul of a nation, is the final step in the moral degradation which is the inevitable accompaniment of a prolonged war.

CHAPTER III

THE ACID TEST

THIS survey of war-idealism shows us everywhere the spectacle of the selfish interests, passions and prejudices of individuals, groups and classes, adopting and exploiting the ideals of self-determination, economic equality and pacific internationalism, in order to defend themselves and to gain further means of satisfaction.

The Peace Treaties are one elaborate travesty of this war-idealism. In substance the resultant of a prolonged series of deals, directed by motives of territorial and economic greed, vengeance and forcible guarantees against the military and industrial recovery of the conquered countries, they have given rhetorical lip-service to these ideals, wherever such formal acknowledgment did not interfere with the plucking of the fruits of victory.

The liberation of subject nationalities by the application of self-determination is claimed as the directing principle in the political reconstruction of Central and Eastern Europe. In no single instance is this claim clearly vindicated. The restoration of Poland, the establishment of Czecho-Slovakia and Jugo-Slavia, the enlargement of Roumania, Italy and Greece, is in each case accompanied by additions of territory torn from their former political allegiance without the consent of their population in order to feed the imperialistic ambitions or the military power or the economic greed of the recipient State. In some instances provisions for a sham plebiscite[1] are given, but in the leading instances even this pretence of self-determination is denied.

The deliberate destruction of the nationality of Albania and the parcelling out of its constituent parts among Jugo-Slavia, Greece and Italy, and the annexation of the Austrian Tyrol are violations of the principle so naked and so violent as to evoke no specious defence in any quarter. But the classical example of the betrayal of self-determination is the denial to truncated Austria of the right to make any political association with Germany, though such association may be indispensable to the subsistence of her population, bereft of access to their former sources of national supplies.

Everywhere the principle of nationality is crossed and compromised by considerations of "historic rights," "economic necessity," military defence, and secret treaty obligations extorted during the war as blackmail. It is characteristic of the moral obliquity of war that the only two examples of the violation of this central principle to which the statesmen and peoples of the Allied countries have turned their serious attention are the Adriatic settlement and the cession of Shantung, the two leading cases where one ally has been wronged in favour of another. To the score of equally culpable instances where wrong has been done to our late

[1] No plebiscite can be a genuine act of self-determination unless it is conducted under neutral supervision, free from enemy occupation and from threats or bribes relating to tariffs, remission of indemnity or other favourable or unfavourable economic conditions.

enemies by a violation of the pledges by which we induced them to surrender our war-idealists have been quite indifferent.

This is not deliberate dishonesty. It is the almost unbridgeable chasm between the mind represented by war-idealism and that represented by a victorious settlement. The principle of self-determination was ousted in application to the several concrete problems of the settlement because it had no real bite upon the mind of the men at Paris. They had all employed it for war-rhetoric to generate enthusiasm and passion. The statesman is usually a man who believes what he says, not one who says what he believes. These men, as they repeated the fine phrases about "a war to end war," to establish democracy and to liberate subject peoples, were no more insincere than the actor who "throws himself into his part" and feels the passions which he undertakes to represent. But such acceptance is a sorry guarantee of performance. These supermen at Paris had, like most statesmen, taken their ideals lightly, for what they were worth. And they were worth something, as we have seen, both for "enthusing" their friends and for weakening the resistance of the enemy. To say that, having squeezed this use from them, they were ready to throw them away and to revert to a different set of motives for making terms of peace, would be too crude an account of the process of evaporation that took place.

The imperfections of war-idealism were of two kinds, illustrated respectively in the conduct of Mr. Wilson and of Mr. Lloyd George. Mr. Wilson took his ideals so seriously, associated them so closely with his personality, desired so insistently their attainment, that it became impossible for him to recognize or acknowledge their failure. The thin formal cloak of principle which wrapped the naked aggressions and spoliations of the treaty sufficed to ward off his closer scrutiny and to enable him to assure himself—or others—that all his points of principle were incorporated in the terms of peace. He must have had qualms and spasms of suspicion, but the urgent moral need for being right and seeing right prevail persistently checked the temptation to look facts squarely in the face. This refusal honestly to test the substance of the victory for his ideals was the method and the measure of Mr. Wilson's insincerity. It found critical expression in his attitude towards the Covenant of the League. Many of his defenders who are not blinded to the deviations from his principles incorporated in the terms of peace, contend that the President either unwittingly or wittingly condoned these faults because of his deep concentration upon the League as the sole security for civilization and the sufficient remedy for any temporary defects in the terms of peace.

The self-consecrated saviour of the world simply could not face the inscription on his memorial tablet "Infectus rediit." So he returned bowing his back beneath the burden of his accomplishment. A sight indeed for God and man! His return to America carrying this stillborn deformed infant is perhaps the most pathetic spectacle in modern history. For this League had hardly a single lineament to identify it with that great Society of Nations which Mr. Wilson beheld in his prophetic vision. It was not a League of Peoples, but a League of Governments. But not of all Governments. It was a League of the dominant war-allies, inviting at their arbitrary will the adhesion upon terms of permanent inferiority of a certain number of "good" neutrals. The structure of the League was such as to assign the determination of all critical issues to the chief war-allies, and a primary avowed object was to maintain the unjust and dangerous territorial changes laid down in the terms of a dictated peace. Upon the war-allies, and their nominees controlling the assembly, devolved the right to accept or reject future applicants for admission to the League. The equality of economic opportunity, recognized by Mr. Wilson as a first essential of a true Society of Nations, was denied to outsiders, including the countries of the late enemies and Russia. The League, thus fashioned, claimed the right of forcible interference in all quarrels of outsiders, constituting itself a world-government with no right of representation on the part of the governed.

The failure of Mr. Wilson to see these distortions of principles in the League as in the terms of peace is an instructive example of the moral obliquity that accompanies the intense craving for self-justification.

The case of Mr. Lloyd George's war-idealism is different. Mr. George never took these or any other principles very seriously. He is not an unprincipled, but rather a non-principled man. Principles, apart from the useful enthusiasm they evoke in others, have no meaning for him in politics. Politics is a game of short-range expedients, coloured and directed by sympathetic tact. This applies to high as well as low politics. History has taught him no lessons about the evolution of society or general tendencies in human affairs. He must deal with each issue that arises on its own merits and by calculations of present expediency. There is for him no other way. His personality is a power-house of flickering ideals and evanescent enthusiasms. These ideals and enthusiasms are not for realization, but for evoking energy which shall be applied to the matter in hand. So the loftiest rhetoric of war-ideals flowed from his lips when the immediate need was the appeasement of labour troubles and the stimulation of the people to intense production of war materials. He felt these glowing phrases as he spoke them, but he did not mean them, at least in any serious sense of the term "meaning." The elevated sentiments of liberty and justice, the bright images of a land fit for heroes and a world living in amity, touched his sympathy and stirred his imagination as he painted them, but they carried neither intellectual nor moral conviction and no lasting will towards their fulfilment. They were true for him at the moment with such measure of sincerity as his facile and changeable mind was capable of entertaining. He had no sense of shame at the betrayal of these ideals by the Peace of Versailles. For he had long ago permitted these ideals to evaporate and their very memory to perish. A new and base coinage of victory-ideals, designed to stir the lower passions of the people during an electoral campaign, had displaced them before the Paris episode began. Even this debased idealism of retribution and indemnities, masquerading as justice in the autumn of 1919, has already passed into oblivion. The very notion that the vivid rhetoric of war-speeches should carry some later obligation to fulfilment is either unmeaning or ridiculous to a politician of the type of Mr. George.

Among the statesmen of Europe a larger number inclined towards the lighter war-idealism of Mr.

George than towards the heavier brand of Mr. Wilson. For a sympathy with fine ideals, not too deep and binding to hamper a career, is an asset in the struggle of politicians for survival and success. That aspirations for liberty, justice and human good will are in some sense moving forces in "the great heart" of the people is no merely flattering pretence. It is a truth, the nature of which we will presently explore, and it is to the credit of the intelligence of "that crafty and insidious animal the statesman or politician" that he recognizes it, and, being human, shares in it.

The result of this analysis thus far has been to exonerate from the gross charge of hypocrisy, or of fully conscious perfidy, the war-idealists who violated in the conduct of the peace the just and high principles of their war-professions. Their adoption and glorification of these ideals was no doubt facilitated by the tense emotional atmosphere in which they were living, and which brought the mind even of the most austere and coldest politician or publicist into an intimacy with the common mind, thus kindling his feelings with some of that "enthusiasm of humanity" which forms the substance of popular idealism. In some such experience we may explain how so case-hardened an aristocrat as Mr. Balfour was able to express an enthusiasm for the cause of democracy and a passion to see it prevail in the world.

There was, however, evinced at Paris in the making of the peace a third attitude towards the war-ideals, which was manifestly an unwilling lip-service. For M. Clemenceau, M. Pichon and their entourage, for Signor Sonnino and the other Italian representatives, the war-ideals of the British and

Americans had no intrinsic value, except as they might be useful to evoke and maintain the war-spirit of sentimentalists and moralists. They were realists for whom "a war to end war," "a peace of justice" and "a new international order" had no significance. A good peace was one which, if possible, would leave them permanently stronger than their vanquished enemies, and would secure for them the territorial and other spoils they coveted and which were the rights of the victors. Whether Clemenceau believed that the array of idealistic and Utopian Points and Principles, and the League of Nations to be based upon them, was an elaborate display of Anglo-Saxon hypocrisy or a tissue of amiable illusions, it is perhaps unprofitable to discuss. But the lip-service he rendered was so palpably perfunctory, so evidently a humouring of the Anglo-American sentimentalism, that it cannot merit serious reprobation. M. Clemenceau never entertained and so never betrayed the great war-ideals. If he sometimes used their language, he scarcely troubled to conceal his contempt for their contents. If in the settlement he left the husks of these ideals, having eaten out the grain, this was a deception for which he entertained no qualms of conscience. It was the tribute that realism must always pay to sentimentalism.

These three men may fairly be taken to impersonate the different attitudes and appeals of war-idealism. In Britain and America the general mind, subjected to the emotional stresses of the war-time, so far as it consciously concerned itself with ideals, took various positions between that of Mr. Wilson and that of Mr. George. "Realists" of the French order were comparatively few. A considerable body of religious or political enthusiasts shared Mr. Wilson's fervour of faith in a new world order. But most took their acceptance of these fine ideals lightly, with Mr. George, retaining all the while those fears, hates, greeds, suspicions and cravings for vengeance which were destined to convert the actual terms at Paris into a "peace of violence" and to reduce the League of Nations to a travesty of internationalism.

But it should not be ignored that the actual settlement not merely retained as much as sophistry could devise of the loftier idealism, but that the separatist, vindictive, and rapacious provisions which formed its substance themselves appealed to a lower level of idealism figuring as Nationalism, Imperialism and Patriotism. Only when one penetrates these disguises does one reach the real interests and sentiments, personal, class or economic, which worked for their own ends under the protective colouring of these more passionate ideals.

The typical example of such handling of ideals in English politics has been the campaign of propaganda by which definite business interests exposed to keen foreign competition have laboured for a protective tariff under the sentimental banner of imperialism. To impute a clearly conscious purpose to these plays of instinctive group-selfishness, and to the primitive passions which crave expression, not only betokens a slipshod psychology but is a dangerous tactical mistake from the idealist standpoint. For most of these persons have succeeded in persuading themselves that they are largely, if not mainly, actuated by unselfish motives in taking lines of conduct serviceable to their private interests. No doubt there exist clearsighted business men whose zeal for a protective tariff that will put money into their pockets is untinctured by any pretence that such a policy is "good for the country." But the vast majority are able to feel indignant at such a charge of selfishness, because it has been easy for them to adopt a line of reasoning which reconciles their personal gain with what appears to them to be the economic welfare of their country.

Among the votaries of aggressive imperialism are many groups of influential business men and politicians whose trade interests or investments have visibly influenced the foreign and imperial policy of this country, but whose convictions and sentiments about "England's mission" in the civilization of the world, by the Christianization and elevation of the backward peoples, are held with real fervour. Charge such persons with hypocrisy, the charge carries no sting; it is indignantly rejected, not only by them, but by all who know them, as a malicious calumny. For hypocrisy it is not. It is selfishness transfigured by a process of protective coloration in which the hidden spring is so habitually kept out of mind that the owner forgets or belittles its existence. In the adoption and practice of this economy there is and must be some measure of insincerity, but the sophistication is far too delicate to be described correctly by any such simple term as that too commonly employed. Moreover, it will be impossible to bring home to the subject the actual vice of this insincerity until it is treated with more sympathy and understanding than the standard indictment of imperialism shows. For unless you can bring home the charge to a man's own conscience, you can achieve nothing in his reformation, and to bring a charge which is felt to be false and is actually false strengthens the self-defence which the accused makes at the bar of his own conscience.

For the same reason the cruder and more violent Socialism has always failed to convict Capitalism in the judgment of the majority of the educated and more open-minded middle classes. The crudeness of its analysis and the extremity of its attack have always played into the hands of the defence. The cardinal error is a failure to perceive and to present the delicate interplay of motives which forms the staple of the great moral drama.

The reactionary elements in every country sustain their private interests in property and economic dominion under the genuine conviction that they are defending the fabric of society. In the sacred name of Law and Order they repress all attempts, peaceable as well as forcible, to subvert, reform or even criticize the pillars of that social fabric. Protectionism appears to them an aspect of patriotism, militarism a purely defensive use of force, and imperialism an extension of the bounds of civilization. Selfish reactionism will not work without some alloy of these finer and more disinterested motives. The economy of enlightened revolution demands a fair recognition of the reality of these finer ideals. They are not mere pretences, nor are they always feeble in the volume of their emotional appeal. Among the foremost exponents of British imperialism are men who have no business axe to grind and who are convinced that the unselfish idealism which inspires them is the dominant directive motive in the imperialist policy. In varying measures this disinterested spirit merges with the complex of economic interests, political ambitions and the disease of territorial aggrandizement, which are the true moulding and determinant forces. It is not even necessary to contend that the idealist motives are inferior in volume or strength. The indictment of imperialism as a reactionary anti-social policy rests upon the charge that the idealism is not the practical controller of the policy but an adjunct and a useful instrument in the hands of the economic and political empire-makers.

And this interpretation is also applicable to other departments of social conduct. Nor can the cynic be permitted to argue that the finer ideals are merely tools. They are neither illusions nor purely passive instruments. They have a reality and some influence of their own, capable sometimes of modifying or deflecting the play of the interestocracies that normally dictate the policies. The logic of capitalism and of imperialism is everywhere impaired in the clearness of its working by concessions made to humanitarianism and sentimentalism. This is often made a topic of scornful grievance by the ideologists of revolution, who recognize how difficult it is to make their theories of the tyranny of capital square with the plain facts accessible to the ordinary worker. Humanitarian concessions they resist as an attempt to buy off justice by charity, and they represent the policy as a conscious cunning of the enemy.

There is no such fully conscious cunning in the matter. And yet, in the defence of capitalism, as in the furtherance of imperialism, this humanitarian alloy of idealistic motives does serve to give cover to the determinant selfish motives. Nor can it rightly be pretended that the defenders are unaware of the services rendered by this idealism in obscuring the play of economic interests. The millionaire monopolist who endows schools and hospitals, the trust which gives most favoured conditions to its employees, the profit-sharing schemes which insert a vertical wedge into the solidarity of trade-unionism, the proposals for promoting peasant-ownership at home or in the overseas Empire, are recognized by their advocates as useful in allaying popular discontent and resentment against great wealth.

To meet and even to anticipate the demands of justice by a less costly policy of voluntary concessions is the typical defence of British conservatism. It is carried from the realism of economics into that of politics. The series of progressive enlargements of the franchise which formally assign to the poorer classes, who form the permanent majority of the electorate, the determination of governments and legislation, while they reserve to the present rulers the real levers of political power, is an example of this concessive policy.

This is not a clearly contrived plan of defence for the ruling and possessing classes. Each step in this "democratic" progress has been accompanied and inspired by a genuine sentiment in favour of fuller popular self-government. But at the same time, a sense of the utility of conciliating popular sentiment by giving a formal extension of power, curbed by a real control over its abuses, has been present in the consciousness or subconsciousness of the conservative classes. They have even pretended to frighten themselves by visions of the perils of mob-rule as an inoculation against the disease itself. The recent scare of Bolshevist and "red" revolution, sedulously sown in Britain and America by the "capitalist" Press, is an interesting instance of the prophylactic virtue of this "make-believe." The menace is not real, nor is it seriously believed to be real by the makers of the propaganda, but the fear thus engendered in the dupes of the propaganda is designed to mobilize the resistance to the more peaceable forms of social-economic revolution which are genuinely feared by the propertied and ruling classes. But everywhere in the psychology of this defence there is an obscurity and a mixing of motives, which is felt somehow to be serviceable to the maintenance of the *status quo*.

. . . . .

If this conclusion be correct, it signifies some semi- or subconscious recognition of the truth and efficiency of those social ideals which conflict with the " interests " of the existing economic and political rulers. The tribute rendered to the high ideals, alike in international politics and in the economic and political struggles within each nation, is itself, as we see, a sufficient refutation of the crude cynicism which professes to regard these ideals as mere illusions, impotent in the determination of human history.

Thus, returning to the drama of war-idealism, we may seek further light upon the crushing defeat of idealism by realism, or, if it be preferred, of the higher, broader and more lasting ideals by the lower, narrower and more immediate. For the *sacro egoismo* of Signor Sonnino and the " Carthaginian peace " of Clemenceau are themselves idealisms of a sort. What, then, is the nature of the higher idealism, and what the purposes or tendencies it serves to promote in the field of action ? And how do these differ from the play of those narrow instincts, impulses or desires which appear so often to keep it in subjection ?

CHAPTER IV

THE ROOTS OF IDEALISM

IN attempting a solution of the problem of political idealism, it is first necessary to revert to the psychology of individual conduct. For the part played by rational idealism in personal conduct is well recognized. It consists in the conscious realization of the personality conceived as a human unit, single, complete and continuous, by securing the dominion of that personality over the desires and impulses which seek severally to seize the reins of government and work their particular satisfaction. This personal idealism is self-control carried from the region of a protective instinct into that of a conscious rational purpose. But here at the outset it is right not to overstate the opposition between the play of the separate instincts and desires and this fuller realization of the self. The self-restraint involved in the denial of free play to each passing impulse ranks in the first instance as a purely biological condition of survival for the individual and the species. It belongs to the economy of organic life. A savage is often envisaged as a man who, like other animals, lives by his passing impulses, with little or no conscious provision for the future. But his actual life is full of restraints, precautions and provisions for his early needs, impelled by what we call the self-protective instincts. Early civilization consists largely in improving, prolonging and making more conscious the operations of these self-protective instincts. Similarly with the family and tribal instincts by which the organic species provides for its survival. Parental love and self-sacrifice for the young we may regard as blind instincts imposed as purely biological conditions of specific survival. Similarly, the herd instinct, extending beyond the range of the immediate family, impels individuals to restrain impulses for achieving some separate immediate gain, in order to contribute to the protection of the larger and more continuous life of the herd. Visible in many parts of the organic world, this subordination of narrow short-range selfishness to wider and longer-range interests often assumes elaborate forms of social organization and co-operation entirely within the range of so-called instincts.

Where the biological urgency for such self-restraint is exceedingly intense, the response of the individual is virtually automatic, and is attended by no conscious choice and therefore by nothing corresponding to a moral struggle. When to automatic instincts are attached definite emotions and desires, there is much to show how incomplete is this automatic response and how often short-range cravings cross and impair the specific interests. It is pretty clear that, in the animal that devours its young instead of fostering them, there has taken place something of the nature of a conflict with some attendant consciousness, conceivably some thin sense of wrong-doing. These beginnings of a moral struggle are, of course, seen more clearly in the breaches of imposed and accepted discipline by dogs, horses and other domesticated animals. So we come to the case of civilized man, in whom the instinct of mutual aid has been transformed into a consciously accepted principle of personal and social behaviour. In other words, we have passed from the realm of instincts to that of ideals. This passage has not been sudden but continuous, and it is important to remember that the highest principles of personal and social idealism are always directed along lines of definitely biological survival. It is even doubtful whether this statement should be modified by adding to the term " survival " the term " progress," in view of the growing complexity of social structure and behaviour that is termed civilization. For the growing process of complexity has itself been a condition of survival. We must " march " in order to hold our ground.

The importance of retaining in moral and political philosophy the clear recognition that we are dealing with conduct which continues ever to be directed by biological considerations of survival is that only thus can we grasp the substance and vitality of ideals.

For if we regard them as pure products of rational consciousness, of a moral and intellectual nature supervening upon our animal inheritance, it is easy for the materialist, the economist, the realist in politics, to dismiss them as illusions or shadowy epiphenomena. But if we recognize that the stuff out of which these ideals, even the loftiest and most spiritual, have been generated is not of ultimately diverse nature from the animal desires and the selfish cravings with which these ideals seem to conflict, the charge of unreality collapses.

Now, the very fact that the war-realists of every country make strenuous efforts to enlist the emotion of the "ideal" in the cause of every modern war is itself a significant testimony to the truth of this presentment. Every great war-statesman recognizes that it is not enough to base his appeals for national support upon the gains which a successful war will bring in territory, trade, power and prestige to large classes of the people, or even to confine himself to rallying the gregarious feelings for collective self-defence. "Your country in danger" is not enough. The war must be presented as a "holy war" for large human purposes of freedom and progress that transcend the limits of the nation. These very ideals which are to be superseded in the hour of victory are recognized as assets in the actual "moral" of a warring nation. The generous youth of every nation responded to the appeal of these ideals, which, blended freely with the craving for adventure, the fighting lust and the various social and economic pressures, served to evoke the enthusiastic answer to the call to arms. Soldier and civilian alike fought and worked for victory the better because some sense of the inherent justice of their cause and of the welfare of humanity was alive in their breast.

Why, then (to return to our crucial issue), is it that these wider and loftier ideals appear to fail in actuality? If they, and the tendency or purpose they incorporate, are in reality the wider interests of a self-protective and progressive humanity, if they represent the specific welfare as distinguished from the individual and group interests, why do they allow themselves to be defeated?

The answer to this question becomes intelligible

by reverting to the narrower arena of personal conduct. Why does what we call our "higher nature" so often succumb to the temptations of our "lower nature," why do our bodily desires, or our short-range impulses, so frequently triumph over our rational self? It is not because, when fairly pitted against one another in a "moral struggle," the lower motives prove themselves stronger than the higher. It is because they employ a rush tactics that carries us away before the moral forces of our personality are fully mobilized. The "irrational" instincts get their work in quicker: the processes of reflection and self-realization involve delay, and this delay is often fatal. This is the inevitable risk of idealism when pitted against the "realism" of the passions and desires which spring more directly from the life of instinct.

The true moral struggle is not the direct conflict between the forces of the animal and of the rational self, but the preliminary struggle for the period of delay needed to secure the mobilization of the rational self.

It is precisely this consideration that gives validity to the governing idea in the proposal of a League of Nations. That scheme cannot seriously pretend that the general will-to-peace shall always prove stronger than that will-to-war which is embedded so deeply in the instinct of man. What it endeavours to secure is the period of delay and of enlightenment which shall give the opportunity for a full rally of the resources of informed public opinion on the side of peace. For the essence of this policy is not, as is sometimes held, disarmament or even the substitution of judicial settlement for war, but simply delay in the forcible execution of the national will.

Hitherto the passion of honour or vital interests, or of revenge or national aggrandizement, has insisted upon immediate action when it has been roused. As in the moral struggle of the individual man, it has fought against delay and reflection, because it has instinctively known that "rush tactics" are favourable to its satisfaction, and that all attempts to scrutinize its claims or to subject them to consideration are likely to impede or thwart the play of passion. It is for this reason that the friends of a League of Nations may do well to confine their early efforts to inducing the several nations to bind themselves, not to abandon war, but to state their case and wait. For the cooling-off time thus secured has its first and chief effect, not in invoking an external interference, but in evoking the play of the reasonable mind of the nation contemplating war. Delay means an appeal from the passion to the reasonable self of a nation. Now, when this appeal is won, this reasonable self will itself enforce the claim for an impartial arbitration and settlement. The stiff fight put up by national pride against submitting any vital interest to outside dictation, the patriotic absolutism to which France and America still profess an unabated allegiance, will be called off so soon as the acceptance of delay makes cooler counsels prevail. For these cooler counsels will carry the elementary truth that no nation (as no man) can be a just judge in his own quarrel. Delay, the statement of the case and the consequent appeal to justice, will, therefore, insensibly and not slowly undermine the absolutism of the modern State, by enabling statesmen to perceive that the reasonable self of a nation can only be maintained by regular effective membership of a

Society of Nations, and that such membership involves a submission of its private arbitrary judgment on international matters of conduct to the rational will of the whole Society. Thus the consent of the members of the League to a period of delay before resorting to armed action is the foundation-stone of the new international order. It is the real victory of reason and justice over force and the separate will-to-power.

Powerful passions moving instinctively, accurately and unswervingly along a single narrow track enjoy a perpetual advantage over the forces of idealism and rationalism. And this is particularly true of collective as distinct from personal conduct. For the passions sweeping over the herd-mind of a people carry an intolerance of that very process of delay and of reflection needed to give the forces of reason their chance. To reflect, to question, to delay, becomes disloyalty. This bestowal of the sham idealism of loyalty or patriotism as a screen for the violent and immediate indulgence of the instincts of hate, fear and combativeness is a remarkable example of protective coloration.

It is often contended that this intolerance, this further repression of criticism, has a biological survival value. But this contention is exceedingly shallow, inasmuch as it ignores the changes that have taken place in the character and methods of war. This instinct for absolute unity and the intolerance it carried with it had doubtless a true biological utility under the simple and brief conditions of a primitive tribal conflict. But the successful conduct of a prolonged and highly complex modern war, in which sober reasoning alike on policy and strategy must be applied at a thousand points, demands the retention and free exercise of the critical faculty. The sham unity of thought and feeling, which intolerance and repressive loyalty seek to enforce, is a source not of strength but of weakness in a modern struggle. The efficient regimentation of the German lay mind into a flat uniformity of thought and feeling was undoubtedly a cause of those grave psychological errors in the conduct of the war which contributed to the military downfall of Germany.

CHAPTER V

THE VINDICATION OF IDEALISM

WE are now in a position to understand the debacle of idealism at Paris. Mr. Wilson's Points and principles failed of realization in the terms of peace and in the Covenant, not because they were found to be Utopian or unjustifiable, but because the conditions of the moral struggle were unfavourable. Each group of allied statesmen came there flushed with complete victory and with the aims, desires and ambitions which such a victory seemed to make attainable. The primitive passions which had found extravagant vent in five years of war were still uppermost and were clamorous to put their own unchecked interpretation upon victory. Reason was at its lowest ebb: idealism could secure no more than perfunctory lip-service.

Versailles reverted to a group of victorious cave-dwellers champing the bones of their slaughtered enemies and wrangling over the loot. Their meagre tribute to idealism consisted in certain pious incantations announcing the righteousness of their intentions, and some skilful rhetoric in the Peace Terms designed to conceal the naked betrayal of the pledges which had secured the enemy's surrender.

. . . . .

This ransacking of the annals of war experience, so far from justifying the belief that short-range passions and interests are the final arbiters of human destiny, the sole determinants of human history, gives a new substance to idealism and to the " progress " of which it is the servant.

For the very abuse and apparent failure of this idealism have enabled us to discover in it qualities of biological as well as ethical value. It represents the deeper-laid, wider and more abiding tendencies, or purposes, of nature in the evolution of human life, as contrasted with the shorter, quicker and shallower instincts and passions which form the psychic equipment of the individual man in the pursuance of his separate personal ends.

Our analysis of the moral struggle, alike in personal conduct and in politics, presents these ideals as the urge of vital forces in man making for a fuller and more rational life. By this fuller and more rational life I signify, first, the realization of the human personality as an organic whole, as distinct from the unordered life resulting from the control of conduct by the several instincts and emotions. Secondly, this rational idealism implies the cooperation of one personality with others in membership of a society continually widening so as to comprise in closer contacts the entire body of contemporaneous mankind, while continually extending its outlook, so as to pay regard to the more distant welfare of humanity.

The rooting of this idealism in physical instincts which, slowly and gradually gathering consciousness, lay claim to sovereign control in the ordering of human conduct, is the guarantee of the reality of human progress. Most of the strong primitive instincts, e.g. of pugnacity and of flight, of self-assertion and self-abasement, of curiosity and of constructiveness, together with the emotions that spring out of them, are primarily engaged in safe-guarding and advancing the life of the individual man, and are only of racial or social value in a secondary sense. But there are others, in particular the parental and the gregarious instincts, with the sympathetic emotions which they carry, that seem primarily designed to conserve and advance the vital interests, not of the individual in which they are manifested, but of the species to which he belongs. In a word, they have social value for survival and progress. No doubt these instincts, involving as they often do efforts and sacrifices of the individual for lives outside his own, are found strongly implanted in low organisms, where they may carry no conscious feeling or definite emotion. But none the less it is to their specific impetus and its utility that we must rightly look for our explanation of the conservation and progress of a species. The sexual and parental instincts in the higher mammals, with the tenderness and sympathy that flow from them, are the beginnings in that enlargement of the personality which, when it attains a wider scope, becomes society. The precise part played by the parental or family feelings in forming the wider and more distinctively social sense of the tribe or horde may well be matter for controversy. But that the tenderness and sympathy within the narrow family circle are educative towards the wider social feeling can hardly be disputed.

The part played by the gregarious instinct in the evolution of the social structure and conduct is manifest. The huddling together of cattle for protection against wind or cold or against beasts of prey, their co-operation in hunting and in migratory movements, may seem to carry no conscious purpose or emotion and to be merely automatic adjustments motived by purely individual feelings of fear or greed. But very low down in animal life we find a negative testimony to gregariousness, as an emotion, in the perceptible distress of animals which have got separated from the herd. In man, at any rate, this gregarious instinct soon has attached to it emotions of an overwhelming strength. In primitive society the customs which spring out of it and the sentiments it inspires are often so predominant as almost to stifle the individual variations of feeling, thought and action upon which social progress depends. All progress, we are told, is due to individual originality, initiative which has escaped the repression and levelling influence of the herd. A free society, it is urged, is one in which law and custom sit lightly on the individual and where full opportunities are afforded for the expression of those tastes which are "egregious." The intolerance of the war-spirit, as we saw, was especially exhibited in the enforcement of herd-mandates.

But the new realization of the importance of individual freedom from these experiences of the persecuting pressure of the herd-mind, masquerading as loyalty and patriotism, must not be allowed to stampede us into a repudiation of all social authority and restraint.

The biological utilities of mutual aid, for the preservation of individual and group life, regarded in the first instance as instinctive urges, bearing some more or less distinct emotional stresses, become, when carried into the realm of thought, social ideals. Idealism begins with the conscious practice of the art of conduct, with the vision of a life beyond the satisfaction of immediate impulse. In every act it involves a conscious and continuous control of those instincts which aim at a separate short-range satisfaction. It subjects the short blind impulses to a wider regimen, designed in the interest of the whole personality. This idealism may be purely self-regarding, as it is with many artists. But the specific instincts in humanity will always be counterworking this narrow personal economy, by pressing the claims of the social whole.

That these social instincts, and the loyalties and ideals which flow from them, work through a series of concentric circles of widening area and weaker feeling, from the close circle of the home to the wide limits of humanity, is a familiar image. Almost the whole of the art of conduct, personal and collective, consists in the adjustment of the several claims of these pressures and loyalties.

It is, indeed, this process of adjustment which first brings out in consciousness the significance of the social instincts and emotions. The respective duties of a man towards himself, his family, his city, his country, humanity, and the cross-loyalties towards craft, church, and other institutions, which form so large a part of modern problems, troubled primitive or even mediæval man very little. They were pretty closely fixed by law and custom: the social feelings ran in narrow prescribed channels and could hardly be said to carry ideals.

The conscious cherishing of political and social ideals, such as nationality, empire, socialism, internationalism, democracy, as distinct from the active unconscious pressure towards these ends, is a very modern process and is still confined to a comparatively small section of the more intellectually and morally alert among the civilized peoples.

But this, as we have recognized, does not mean that the popular appeal to ideals was a merely decorative decency of politicians. The rhetoric about the destruction of militarism, the enthronement of public law, the establishment of democracy, had indeed no intellectual or moral meaning for the masses. But the appeal to national defence and to the punishment of outrages against humanity deeply stirred those latent instincts of gregariousness and sympathy which furnish the emotional contents of ideals. Millions of men, to whom patriotism or any other "ism" had never presented itself for feeling or consideration, came to realize their country, the Empire, the cause of the Allies, as live, real objects of reverence, ideals for which they were willing to fight and work and pay. So this latent loyalty to ideals became actual. The contents of these ideals were vague and inchoate, but the passions were intense.

Here we strike the greatest of the perils which the experience of war-idealism discloses. The intelligent and emotional susceptibility of the peoples in modern civilized countries has been educated up to that level which affords to interested traders in idealism dangerous opportunities of exploiting "the emotion of the ideal" for their private ends.

CHAPTER VI

THE EXPLOITATION OF IDEALS

THE exploitation of the herd-instinct and herd-loyalty for selfish purposes is, of course, as old as man himself. The male head of the family, the patriarch, diverted to his personal comfort, power and glory, the devotion and subservience of his wives and children, designed for the prime purpose of co-operation for racial survival. The cave-man did this. The Zulu does it still. The modern "gentleman" continues the tradition, though he tends to use his family for decorative contribution to his personal pride more than for laborious utility. But the original abuse strongly survives in the working-class family of most European countries, where wife and children are still realized as economic assets, their personal interests and needs subordinated to those of the head of the family.

The most momentous example of the exploitation of specific for individual purposes is, however, furnished by the distinctively modern practice of limitation of the family. Here, however, we should be upon our guard. For the blend of motives inducing restraints of the birth-rate contains factors favourable as well as detrimental to specific survival and progress. A measure of purposive limitation is not only defensible in the legitimate interests of the individual members of the family, parents and offspring alike, but, by substituting qualitative for quantitative human values, it may contribute to a general rise in the standard of life and character for the whole community.

But though it may be granted that the better life from a smaller family and a less numerous community furnishes a valid defence for some restriction, it cannot seriously be held that the normal prompting motives to restriction have these conscious contents. The refusal of the burden and the risks of a family is usually motived, less by consideration for the interests of the children to whom birth is denied, or of the community which may be benefited by a lower population, than by the narrowly personal consideration of parents for their own ease. Now, while it may well be true that such reasonable or even selfish considerations may rightly weigh against the wasteful pressure of an unregulated racial instinct, there is nothing in the present play of motives to secure a good adjustment between individual and racial claims. The instability of social-economic arrangements in most civilized countries prompts to a restriction of the birth-rate in every class sufficiently educated to exercise any regular control over the primary human instincts. The net result of what is happening is to reduce the number of those stocks within each nation, and throughout the world, which develop most capacity of rational self-control. It is not merely that the most "successful" classes refuse to contribute their share to the upkeep of the race. For it might be racially advantageous that some of the qualities contributing to success in a woefully unequal struggle, directed to low standards of success, should be bred out. But it is manifestly true that the finest individual types of men and women, morally, intellectually and even physically, in every walk of life appear unwilling to reproduce their kind. This appears to make for racial deterioration. It may no doubt be urged that in the long run Nature will take care of herself, and that the breeding out of stock in which personal comfort is a stronger incentive than "racial duty" is advantageous from the standpoint of humanity. But the sacrifice of the otherwise finest fruits of humanity in the process is a terrible cost to pay. Is it necessary or inevitable? Is it not in the last resort a selfish egoism? Organic nature everywhere produces individual organisms and careers as the means of securing specific survival and growth. For individuals to apply to their own private exclusive advantage and satisfaction faculties and resources thus "intended" as aids to the performance of their specific duty is clearly a betrayal of humanity. The individual becomes a parasite upon the species, exploiting its resources for his private gain.

Primitive man bred freely, giving free vent to the specific instinct for survival with which he is endowed. His abuse consisted in an excessive subordination of the good of the family to his own private ends. This attitude still survives in those communities, or classes, where the social situation retains a family as an economic asset exploitable by the dominant male. But where the family passes from the credit to the debit side of the account, becoming a burden rather than a source of strength, the spirit of exploitation turns against the production of a family and the reproductive instincts are devoted to barren modes of satisfaction.

The rationalization of this parasitism by Neo-Malthusianism is the first scene in the elaborate comedy of ideals by which selfishness seeks to clothe itself in robes of righteousness, and claims to be actuated in its self-regarding conduct by high considerations of the good of humanity.

It may, however, be admitted that this exploitation of wider by narrower interests and instincts is mainly conducted below that level of consciousness with which we are concerned in our study of idealism. Its importance consists in illustrating our contention that the conflict between individual and specific instincts, purposes and ends is the key to the understanding of human history.

The open comedy of idealism is exhibited in the exploitation of herd instinct and loyalty throughout the wider fields of politics. As we pass from the simple tribal organization of primitive man, with its strong instinctive unity and loyalty, to the enlarging and elaborating structure of modern society, we do not escape the conflicts of forces working for racial evolution and those working for personality within the race. On every plane the grouping of individuals by occupation, locality, political opinions, religion, social status or other community of interest, exhibits the same problems of conduct. Associations, formed primarily and avowedly for the common good, breed attachments and loyalties. The herd-instinct breathes into the club, party, town, church, movement, an *esprit de corps* strengthened by contacts and co-operation. This spirit forms the emotion of the ideal to which formal intellectual expression may be given in programme, creed or other statement of aims. This idealism of purpose makes the "soul" of the institution, it furnishes the fund of operative energy, and, so far as it remains pure and flows freely, the grouping subserves the interest of humanity. But everywhere it is liable to two perversions. Selfish individuals or cliques may divert the stream of loyalty to turn their private wheels. The politician "on the make" and the "social climber" are familiar examples of this abuse. Here the individual member may be said to live parasitically upon the life of the social institution. But the perversion more significant for our purpose, as involving the graver abuse of its "idealism," arises where the party, church, trade or other grouping itself gives a false expansion to its ideals, and usurps the place of a wider social grouping with a larger loyalty. The claim of a party, or a pushful group of politicians or of trading interests, to represent the nation in the conduct of national politics is, of course, the commonest example of this abuse. This does not simply mean that a section of the nation, having some particular objects to serve, goes outside its province, trespassing upon the wider purposes of the community. It means that it has foisted its narrower collective purpose, and the loyalty appertaining thereto, into the place which properly belongs to the wider purpose and loyalty of the whole community. Nay more than that, it means that certain dominant personal wills within the party, class or economic interest, are enabled, through this illicit expansion of their narrow union, to wield the moral and material resources of a whole people. "Everywhere," wrote More, "do I perceive a certain conspiracy of rich men seeking their own commodity under the name and pretext of the commonwealth." They always operate by seizing the banner of some wider loyalty and enlisting under this stolen emblem the forces of a deluded majority. This is doubtless too simple a psychological analysis, implying in the political exploiters too clear a consciousness of what they are engaged in doing. It is so easy for any dominant desire to rationalize and ennoble its aims, and to accept with genuine conviction its higher mission. The history of nineteenth-century Nationalism is rife with instances of small landowning or other ruling classes riding into domination upon a tide of popular enthusiasm for liberty. But the culminating example is found in that expansive and aggressive Nationalism styled Imperialism. For there is to be found at once the plainest drive of narrow economic motives with the loftiest professions of idealism. To extend the boundaries of civilization, to bring Christ's Gospel to the heathen, to teach the dignity of labour to untutored savages, to bear the White man's burden—such have been the professions under which competing groups of officials, traders and concession-hunters in the several imperialist nations have sought—and not in vain—to conceal from the eyes of others and their own the nakedness of their designs. What one of our great imperialist statesmen of the nineties called "the free, tolerant, unaggressive British Empire" still pursues its expansive career, inspired by the same lofty professions. If the sincerity of these altruistic motives is ever called in question, what is the reply? It is to point to the value of the process, as assessed by the interested parties that engage in it, an extreme form of pragmatism which claims to whitewash past motives with present alleged results. "We must have taken on Egypt for the good of the Egyptians, because you see how much more prosperous the people have been under our sway!"

I am not, however, concerned here with the validity of the imperialist process as tested by its utility, but only with the state of mind which is able to overlay its real motives with this decorative idealism, so as to induce the peoples to sacrifice their lives and money for the benefit of their business rulers. For behind all the recent struggles of the nations has lain this real motivation. And when the true history of the Great War has been rescued from the clutches of time-serving and patrioteering historians, to be presented in its deeper origins, it will stand out as the culminating act in the clash of interests among the little economic groups which were in control of the political levers in their respective countries and were able to present their profitable needs under the guise of "national defence." These knots of powerful men were able to evoke and exploit the latent enthusiasms which the herd-instinct, operating under modern psychological conditions, presents as national ideals. Intended by nature for the preservation of the species, they were thus turned to its destruction.

Such is the tragi-comedy of war-idealism, which has driven so many to despair or to protective cynicism. But there is no warrant for such pessimism when we realize the origin and nature of the ideals. For the social instincts of which they are the conscious expression are endowed with a permanent survival value that is transmitted to the ideals themselves. The perversions to which those ideals are exposed themselves testify to their reality and permanence. The struggle towards a happier, securer and freer social order consists in rescuing these instincts and their ideals from the clutches of parasitic individuals and groups, in order to place their life-preserving and life-raising virtues at the common disposal of the human race, through ever larger, closer, securer and more numerous associations.

PART IV

THE NEW INDUSTRIAL REVOLUTION

CHAPTER I

THE CHALLENGE TO PROPERTY

IT was a shrewd instinct of self-defence which led the Governments of the belligerent States to imprison men and women of the working classes who denounced "a Capitalist War." The formal accusation in such cases was that this statement was damaging to the recruiting and discipline of the army. But this was a mere pretext. For, when such cases were on trial, it was seldom thought necessary to adduce any evidence of such damage, nor were the circumstances usually such as to affect either recruiting or discipline. The manifest motive for such prosecutions lay in the genuine feeling of popular outrage against the fouling of a holy cause. The crime was one of treason and of sacrilege. But behind this genuine sentiment of outrage lay an undefined and unexpressed fear. It was a fear for the established order, the capitalist system in politics and industry, lest the war, which had staved off gathering troubles and brought profitable unity to the nation, might, when it ended, leave the ruling propertied classes everywhere exposed to the attacks of a proletarian revolution. It was this sense of wrath to come which more than any other cause led the Governments to shun the making of a clean peace. Behind all the delays and difficulties of conflicting imperialisms and the division of spoils, consecrated under formulas of justice, lay this instinctive repugnance to facing the "revolutionary" music. Even before the Russian Autocracy fell, the rumblings of gathering discontent and the holding up to ransom of the Government by organized labour in munitions and other essential industries worked as premonitory symptoms in this and other countries. But the Russian outbreak in 1917, with its complete destruction of the established order and its dramatic linkage of politics and economics under proletarian domination, was dimly recognized by the Western ruling castes as a grave new peril.

The real significance of the occurrence they could not in the nature of the case recognize. It was to their eyes an outbreak of criminal fanaticism which, favoured by sudden opportunity, secured for a small oligarchy of revolutionary communists a brief reign of terrorism. They would have liked to have stamped it out, but they rightly apprehended that any open and vigorous attempt to do so must react upon their idealistic professions, already exposed to inevitable suspicions among their war-wearied and disillusioned peoples. Thus they dared not make open war. But neither dared they make peace with Bolshevism. Some of their advisers would have them fight and starve it into deeper desperation, in the hope that some stern deliverance would emerge from this extremity in the shape of a strong government able to keep the proletariat in their place and willing to keep faith with Western creditors. But, though they tampered with this policy, they dared not stake enough men and money to give it a full trial. Moreover, so active and costly an intervention would ill accord with their constant professions that Bolshevism was doomed to early collapse by its inherent vices and the gathering resentment of the Russian populace. Hence a limited intervention with a *cordon sanitaire* for the protection of Western Europe against Bolshevist propagandism. This vacillation and delay carried the incidental gain of preserving a state of insecurity which, while not demanding great national expenditure of effort, justified the maintenance of exceptional powers for the respective Governments. It does not belong here to discuss the ethics of the suppression of propaganda, or to expatiate upon the maxim that the best way to kill an error is to expose it to the sun. It suffices to recognize the infatuation of supposing that the forcible suppression of the publication of Lenin's speeches in this country could help the cause of property and social order.[1] The workers of this country are not skilled dialecticians. But when this Government told them in one breath that Bolshevism was doomed to perish because of the falseness of the ideas it pretended to realize, and that those ideas were so dangerous that they must not be allowed to be presented here, their curiosity and interest might well be aroused. But this infatuation was carried a step further when the politicians and the Press of this country, of France and America strove to fasten Bolshevism as an opprobrious label upon the active labour and socialist propaganda in their respective countries. Now, it is important to understand why that teaching seems really dangerous to the ruling propertied

[1] An incident of April 1918.

classes of this country. Its chief danger was not clearly sensed at first; it appeared to lie not in its syndicalism, the displacement of "regional" by "functional" democracy, or even in its proscription of the parasitic classes, but in its doctrine and example of catastrophe as the revolutionary method. The democratic movement in Western Europe since the collapse of 1848 had been moving upon the whole more and more in the direction of reformism and opportunism. Though repressive laws against socialism and anarchism, harshly administered in periods of panic, with occasional exhibitions of the alternate weapon of starvation wielded by capital to crush strikers, always kept alive revolutionary groups to whom force was the midwife of reform, the general tenor of the democratic movement in all Western countries was in fact, if not in principle, one of compromise. The working classes had, after all, been drilled to patience and to moderate expectations by countless generations of subjection, and though a few wild spirits might stir them to demand their kingdom down upon the table, the vision of a proletarian domination issuing from a triumphant violence made no wide or deep appeal. Through the second half of the century the extension of popular representation in the State and the improvements for the skilled workers of their standard of living and conditions of employment had sufficed to stave off any violent assertion of proletarian power. It was partly the sense, sustained by solid facts, that they were gaining ground, with a congenital distrust for violence and for plunges into the unknown, partly a distrust of "thinkers" with their "ideals" and their "Utopias." We have already seen the surprise and the angry sense of bafflement which the new century brought, with its tightening of capitalist control, its gradual reduction of real wages, and its exhibition of the impotence of working-class influence upon the State. Of this last disillusionment there had been striking instances in every country. Socialist and labour parties of considerable numbers had entered the bourgeois Parliaments in every country save America ; a few of their numbers in France and in Britain had even taken office under Governments. Thus Parliamentarism seemed impotent alike to achieve reform or to stay reaction. The current of working-class sentiment and policy began to turn from pacific and constitutional to shock methods, syndicalism was spreading, less in theory than in practice. Evolution was again preparing to put on its red R. But nowhere was there clear intention, nowhere, save in a few almost negligible thinkers, any revolutionary design. "Unrest" was the not inept euphemism which journalists had put upon the general mind. But it was a more positive state than the term implies. It was confusion carrying the elements of social explosion. The safeguard lay in its lack of any general consciousness of purpose or direction. States with their confidence in deep-set stability, governments conscious of their "resources of civilization," did not really tremble before so blind a tumult. Public order was indeed disturbed, the essential processes of economic life were occasionally held up for ransom, property was damaged, Parliament was treated with contempt, labour leaders and trade-union government were flouted by their followers. But these things were not done on principle, there was no governing purpose or clear idea directing them. Therefore, they were not very dangerous. Ideas alone are dangerous, for they alone can give direction.

Now upon this tumult and confusion of thought, feeling and action, fell the war. And from the smoke of war has emerged this monster of Bolshevism. It appears as the only creative product of the war. All else is destruction and dissolution. Bolshevism plainly stands for the new political and economic order in Russia. It claims to be founded upon principles of social justice and utility applied to secure the effective and fruitful fellowship of working men and women in a world where work is needed to win a livelihood from nature. It recognizes only workers as citizens, including those whose work is of their brains, and workers alone are entitled to share the fruits of industry. There is no place in this society for parasites, persons who in virtue of " possessing property " claim to eat without working. Whatever provision is made for feeding, clothing and housing parasites, whose parasitism has disabled them for effective labour, is purely eleemosynary. Such " property " has no rights.

It may be justly said that there is nothing new in these revolutionary ideas. They have been the common stock of socialism for all time. But hitherto they have been empty preachment. Now they come upon us with the *cachet* of achievement. It is true that this achievement may be of brief duration, may be the impudent tyranny of a forcible minority it is declared to be by the Allied Governments and the Russian *émigrés*. But its claim to be the incarnation of the revolutionary idea is not denied. Be it admitted that Soviet government does not spring from the express will of the people, that it originates in a small organized minority of " realists " forcibly stamping their will upon a reluctant or a dubious consent of the people, does not this very fact vouch its legitimacy as an offspring of the war? Force as the instrument of liberty and justice, to make a world safe for democracy, was emblazoned on the banner of the champions of right in the conflict of nations. Under the banner of this ideal (the will of a conscious minority in each Allied country), the peoples waded through torrents of blood to the destruction of German militarism. Victory achieved, what then? The forcible will of the victors imposing liberty and justice on a prostrate, unresisting Europe. If force, wielded by autocratic governments, is the only way of winning liberty and justice for nations, may not, must not, the same instrument serve to win liberty and justice for classes? Must not some nation herald this discovery, and tempt the rest to follow its example? It was neither accident nor genius but dire necessity that made Russia the pioneer. For her the task of breaking German militarism and freeing democracy in Germany gave way before the recognition of the nearer duty of breaking Russian militarism and freeing "democracy" in Russia. Germany was an enemy, and millions of Russian lives were spent in fighting her. But there was for Russians a nearer enemy in Russia, and so a natural economy of force drew it from the distant to the nearer struggle. Military disasters, revelations of Court corruption, of bureaucratic robbery and treason, tolled the knell of Tsardom. But this war-weariness and disillusionment could not have served to extricate Russia from the war had not the force *motif* been furnished with another outlet. The great mass of the Russian people wanted the land with a new intensity bred of the possibility of attainment. The seething proletariat of the towns wanted they scarcely knew what, perhaps the factories and mines and shops—certainly the abolition of masterhood and some tolerable security of livelihood. In the heart of every people at all times has lain this craving for the material conditions of personal freedom and happiness, mostly latent and obscure in expression, but always ready to make some response to the kindling words of the agitator. Overmuch credit perhaps is given to ideologues and their formulas in the economy of revolution. Their destructive logic and their speculative reconstruction have little bite upon the common mind. Not that they are negligible or unnecessary. But their real place is that of supplying kindling words to agitators, who are a type of middlemen, sometimes orators, sometimes journalists, sometimes ordinary men and women with some personality and a social gift. Marxism is the most striking modern instance. Its cold abstract doctrine of the necessary evolution of economic structure and class power, of surplus value and of machine-domination, built on a joint foundation of Hegelian dialectics and generalizations from British modern capitalism, could not directly touch the springs of energy in any people. But it can furnish steel weapons of intellectual confidence to propagandists for the curious processes of argument and refutation which accompany this appeal to the interests and cravings of the people. Curious processes, I call them. But they are not the hollow and dishonest appeals to the baser passions which defenders of the existing order signify by agitation. Such fuel could yield no dangerous fire of revolution. To say it could is a libel on the human race. It would imply a degree of folly and of wickedness in human nature inconsistent with the history of human institutions. A revolutionary movement may be misdirected and betrayed by bad leaders, but its origin cannot lie in malign inventions. "The matter of seditions," said Sir Francis Bacon, "is of two kinds, much poverty and much discontent." To this malady of condition and of feeling the agitator must apply his simple and convincing remedies. Socialism easily explains poverty, and shows how discontent may be removed. But the heart of the people is impatient, and as soon as they are shown the cause and remedy they demand immediate satisfaction. This means revolution by force. In Russia the force was there: a disbanded but sufficiently organized soldiery, inflamed with the destruction of Russian autocracy, was ready to help destroy its political and economic associates, landlordism, capitalism, bureaucracy, nationalism, imperialism. But this, it will be urged, does not explain the peculiar shape of Bolshevism and the just instinct of danger it evokes in the eyes of the Western rulers. When our idealizing statesmen decorated this war with their mottoes of liberty and democracy, they were trading purposely with the language and concepts of the past. They wanted, they explained, a moderate revolution in Germany and Austria, perhaps even in Russia, for the Tsarist rule, though accepted, was not altogether trusted. By a moderate revolution they meant political changes which would establish in these countries the sort of democracy which prevailed in Britain, France and the United States. Monarchy or Republic they rightly recognized as a matter of mere local sentiment or convenience, involving no principle. What they wanted to see established was responsible parliamentary government, a manageable democracy broad-based upon the people's will. Such a democracy experience had taught them was perfectly consistent with, nay, under modern conditions essential to, the survival of Capitalism in the State and in Industry. A widening franchise was no menace to property or class rule. For the art of political management had grown apace. Party, press, pulpit, schoolroom, music-hall, public-house, cinema and every focal point in the administrative machinery, were in their hands. They had seen labour and socialist parties, which had threatened to force working-class control upon parliamentary governments, reduced to impotence. Labour agitations, menacing in their strength and tactics, might surge about the economic pillars outside, but the solidly capitalist State could smile at them undismayed. It might be necessary for capitalism to make concessions to the workers, and in this process State legislation might have to take a hand. But capitalism, every year solidifying its position, could afford such concessions, recouping itself through its tightening control over prices and its transfer of sweated industry from this country to distant lands where it had more freedom to teach to backward races the dignity of labour.

But there was one indispensable condition for the harmony between democracy and capitalism. Democracy must be kept political. Whatever alterations and improvements in democratic machinery were made carried no real menace, provided only that industrial organization did not directly thrust itself on politics. The abolition of all property qualifications, adult suffrage, second ballot, proportional representation, even the referendum and initiative, the extreme forms of democracy, are easily compatible with the maintenance of a capitalist order in Society. Property can always make good its defences, provided that the ultimate basis of representation is locality—that is to say, a basis which excludes close and effective community of economic interests.

The burst of angry clamour against the Soviet idea and the insistence of statesmen and organs of opinion, notoriously undemocratic in their sympathies, upon the moral and political orthodoxy of a constituent assembly chosen by localities had its humour. But it was directed by a just perception that if once the notion of industrial unionism caught on as an electoral idea, capitalist democracy was doomed. It might have seemed at first sight a matter of indifference whether voting took place by trade grouping or by local grouping, provided the same persons voted. It is, therefore, interesting to note with what accuracy of nose the rulers in each Western country scented from afar the mischief of the Soviet system. With one consent they took the rôle of champions of the constituent assembly which the Bolshevist rule had repudiated. For the constituent assembly meant the orthodox political democracy, the innocuous character of which their own experience had attested. It mattered little that they crowned this democratic rôle with the active support of General Denekin, Admiral Kolchak and other reactionary leaders who made no serious pretence of favouring popular self-government. Moreover, their instinct of self-defence made them reluctant to allow the clear issue between political democracy and industrial democracy to present itself to Western peoples. Therefore, they concealed in part their apprehension and resentment of the Soviet form of democracy by charging force and fraud in its application. The Soviet government, they contended, in no way expressed the will or true consent of the people, even in their capacity of workers, but was an iron reign of terror exercised by a small minority of fanatics and criminals through a monopoly of arms and food control. In order to support this contention they maintained a constant barrage of atrocity propaganda in their Press, accompanied by a refusal to allow independent journalists and other visitors to enter Russia, and a prohibition of articles and pamphlets claiming to refute the charges made against the Bolshevists or to present their case. Moreover, every official step was taken to prevent the effective publication of all counter-charges of atrocity brought against the reactionary governments in Russia and Hungary and the White Guards in Finland. By such methods it was hoped that the public uneasiness at their forcible intervention in Russia after " the war was over " would be kept within bounds, and that, with the speedy downfall of this criminal conspiracy, they might still pose as the liberators of the Russian people. To this end they applied two means, armed support to the reactionaries and starvation to the town populace, the conjunction which they supposed might be effective in crushing Bolshevism and so stopping the poison at its source.

Now it is not necessary here to form a judgment regarding the degree of truth in the charges against the Bolshevik rule. That terrible deeds of savagery were committed in this sudden widespread overthrow of Tsardom with its long record of savagery may be taken for granted. It may well be true that force and starvation have been used in the establishment and maintenance of Soviet rule by a class-conscious minority. Neither the theory nor the practice of revolutionism forbids the supposition. On these points of historical moment I make but two comments. First, it is impossible for any reasonable person either to believe or to disbelieve charges of atrocity or tyranny, uttered with whatever authority or with whatever evidence, when he is aware that effective opportunity either of contradiction or of cross-examination is refused. Such statements, by supporters of Bolshevism or by presumedly independent witnesses, as escape the governmental censorship go to discredit the accusations of the enemies of Bolshevism as regards the extent of the violence and the amount of popular support given to that rule. But here again we can feel no confidence. On general grounds I hold it likely that the Russian temper, as disclosed to Western eyes, equally prone to outbursts of savagery and repentance, and steeped in years of physical and moral wreckage, has mingled with its effort at liberation and construction terrible elements of vengeance and ruthlessness. But does that afford even a specious excuse for the Allies to refuse Lenin and Trotsky the countenance they did not refuse to the late Tsar when his hands were dripping with the blood of his people and his agents were stamping out in Russia the beginnings of that constitutional democracy of which these Allied Governments are now the glad patrons?

No. There is only one adequate clue to the Allied attitude. At any cost of life and treasure, of principle, of mere consistency, the Soviet idea must be killed in Russia, Hungary, or elsewhere where it has found lodgment, lest it should move westward. The notion that the enunciation of ideas, true or false, innocent or guilty, can in these days be stopped by a *cordon sanitaire* of censorship seems ridiculous enough when it is formulated. But the Governments are not really guilty of such foolishness. They did not think that their peoples could be ultimately stopped from reading Lenin's speeches or from hearing defences of the Bolshevist experiment. They only hoped to keep out the Soviet propaganda until it came not with the stamp of apparent success but of utter failure. An industrial democracy provided by proletarian revolution must be shown to be impossible. It must be made impossible, if the effort demands an illimitable blockade with its accompanying starvation and the restoration of a reactionary despotism by Allied arms. Such was the dominant policy of the Allied Governments until the summer of 1920, when the approaching menace of starvation not only for Central Europe but for France and Britain, by the collapse of credit for trade with other countries with food and materials to sell, compelled the Western Governments to reluctantly discuss resumption of economic intercourse with Russia, even at the risk of something like a formal recognition of the Soviet Government

Now, why was it a matter of such supreme concern to discredit the Soviet idea and to keep out its propaganda? In the past history of Western politics, and particularly in this country, there has been nothing to suggest the abandonment of the historical development of political democracy in favour of a radically new form. A few years ago it would never have occurred to scent danger from such a quarter. Why does it seem dangerous now? The answer, I think, is not obscure. The working classes in this and other Western countries have in their easygoing and empirical pursuit after better conditions of work and life been forced to halt before economic barriers that are not to be surmounted by the combination of trade-unionism and occasional politics which they had been wont to employ. They have been forced to stop and think. New methods were being canvassed in the years before the war. The syndicalist idea was beginning to ferment in the working-class movement. It was shaping various schemes of industrial unionism and Guild Socialism, based on the proletarian control of the several industries and of the general conditions of economic existence. It was supported by the apparent failure of trade-unionism to make good, and by a disillusionment with the experiment of a Parliamentary Labour Party. The confidence of the workers in the franchise and in parliamentary action, which from the times of Chartism had kept in strong control the forces of revolutionary violence in this country showed signs of exhaustion. The "Capitalist State" was too strongly barred against the workers. They could not hope to control Parliament. Their Labour members in the House of Commons were either drugged or outwitted in the game of politics. They were confronted with a ministerial despotism, grown stronger in each decade, with a Cabinet absolute in its control of legislation. The sometimes real influence which the presence of a Labour Party exercised to check or modify capitalistic measures was hardly apparent to the workers. Moreover, the active grievances of workers in the administration of the laws were unredressed. The selection of a few labour leaders for posts on the Board of Trade, the appointment of a handful of workmen to the magisterial bench, were no real checks upon class government. This was the growing sentiment of the younger workers. In what may be termed the more "class-conscious" quarters of the Clyde, South Wales and parts of Lancashire and the industrial Midlands, a powerful ferment of economic Sinn Fein was seething, the idea of industrial self-determination outside the State. Revolutionary in its reliance upon the strike weapon and eschewing any close constructive policy, it exhibited the general character of French and Italian syndicalism. Sober observers did not rate it very seriously. It was not reasonable to suppose that the British workers, however disappointed with immediate politics, would cut themselves adrift from political methods and in effect declare war upon the existing State. There is no such taint of anarchism in our blood or traditions. But the danger of the spread of Bolshevism seems real to our rulers. For it appears to aim not at the setting up of a separate industrial power over against the political State, but a seizure of that State by shifting its foundation. A State in which the right to vote was confined to recognized "workers," voting not by local but by occupational electorates and returning a Parliament of workmen to use all the constitutional machinery of the making and enforcing of laws, would convert Government from a "manageable" political democracy into an "unmanageable" industrial democracy. The workers in nominal power as inhabitants are found to carry no real menace to property and control of industry. The same workers in real power as delegates of industrial unions present a very different "proposition."

Now, I do not suppose that our rulers and our propertied classes are seriously apprehensive lest Russian Bolshevism *pur et simple* should possess the working-class movement of this country. The notion that a Trade Union Conference, or any powerful workers' Soviet, would formally renounce the existing electoral methods and would improvise the structure of a new industrial State which must come into immediate conflict with the existing political State is not worth a moment's consideration. Yet the only alternative, that Parliament itself should constitutionally shift from its local electoral basis to the new occupational basis, is even less conceivable. The real reason why the Soviet must be discredited is not fear lest we should copy Russia, but lest our working-class movement should take from that experiment a certain element of proletarian strength which, incorporated in our reconstructed State, would be a direct and powerful challenge to the rights of property and the accompanying control of profitable industry. That element, the admission of functional representation into the processes of government, might take various forms. The statutory recognition of craft or of industrial unions as instruments for the settlement of wage-rates or other conditions of employment, or for the administration of unemployed relief, pensions or other legal benefits, is likely to be one path towards a definite status for organized labour in our governmental system. The establishment of representative government within our economic system from the unit of the workshops to the National Industrial Council cannot proceed far without a number of reactions upon the political State. Statutory rights and statutory powers will be needed, demanded and conceded at many points to representative bodies in which organized labour will be able to make good its claims and interests far more effectively than through direct political control.

This new form of representation, substituted for, or supplementary to, the existing form, makes two claims, first that it is more genuinely democratic, secondly, that it makes for greater efficiency of government. The first claim is based upon the contention that common employment is a stronger bond of union than propinquity of dwelling. A working man knows more about his fellow-workers in the same factory, mine, wharf, warehouse or shop than he does about those who live in the same street or ward, and has more in common with them. This closer intercourse and community of interest with fellow-workers are a better education of a common will for purposes of political co-operation than the slighter and more fragile bond of neighbourhood. For modern politics are more and more concerned with economic issues affecting citizens in their capacity as workers. The second claim links up with the first at this point. The economic issues which bulk so big in politics demand for their efficient consideration expert representatives selected from the special industries concerned, not general politicians chosen by a casual group of local voters on mixed qualifications mostly irrelevant to these crucial issues. In support of this contention it is added that the existing system leans heavily upon the side of expert representation of the interests of capital. For, whereas the industrial representation of labour is confined to a small number of constituencies where local happens to coincide with functional representation, as in certain mining, textile and shipping centres, capital in its several specialized interests, industrial, commercial and financial, is represented with an overwhelming preponderance. Direct functional representation alone, it is contended, can redress this balance and give labour its proper place in the settlement of political-economic issues.

The most definite form which the demand for industrial democracy has taken in this country, known as Guild Socialism, seeks to establish at once a separation and an adjustment between industrial and political government. The principle of full self-government in the operation and conditions of industry is to be applied by the grouping of self-governing workshops in district and national guilds for several trades, with the co-ordination of these guilds, under the federal government of a National Guilds Congress. The people, as producers, are to control and determine their conditions of production. But the political State of citizen-consumers, elected as heretofore by localities, is to acquire and own the plant and whole fabric of industry, placing it at the disposal of the Guilds on stipulated conditions for its application to the social service. From industry thus administered the State will draw by Guild taxes the revenue it needs for the work of political government and for such public services as may be recognized as non-economic. The State, moreover, will represent the interests of the consuming public when any conflict of interests may seem likely to arise between producer and consumer in relation to prices and other questions of supply, and a joint conference of the Guild Congress and Parliament would be the first court of appeal in all issues of doubtful areas of control or in all matters where legal procedure or enforcement were required.[1] There are already schisms and sects within Guild Socialism, and many of the relations between industrial and political government are vaguely conceived. Nor can it be said that in any of its presentations it offers any working model of a society in which the economic and the non-economic elements of wellbeing are harmoniously combined. The nearest approach to such harmonious unity is conveyed in the ominous image of a balance of powers. This failure to achieve the conception of organic unity in social self-government is probably inevitable in a procedure avowedly one-sided, in working for the continuous enlargement of self-governing industry up to the points where it comes into actual conflict with the functions of the political State. If the organic union is to be achieved, it demands that the problem of the new social order be realized simultaneously in terms of industry and politics, and that the humanity of the new order represents an equal growth and a community of purpose in the reform of political and economic structure.

But our immediate interest does not lie in the measure of truth, equity or practicability which these schemes may contain, but in the body of testimony they supply to support the view that the war has helped to ripen or precipitate a new era of political society in which the rights of property and the related government of industry are everywhere subject to direct challenge and radical revision.

[1] Mr. G. D. H. Cole's *Self-Government in Industry* (Bell and Son) is the best popular exposition of Guild policy.

Though the proletarian violence upon the Continent is the most drastic display of this new tendency, and the vested interests of property and authority dwell upon it as evidence of the criminality of the tendency itself, these tactics cannot avail to quench the new spirit of inquiry and of social justice kindling everywhere in the minds and hearts of men.

War is itself no nurse of reason, no cleanser of the passions. On the contrary, it inhibits clear thinking, feeds and exercises the baser emotions, and subjects individual personality to the wild dominion of the herd. But when mankind has passed through this debauch and is struggling back to sanity, war may be at once a revelation and a liberation. In millions of minds to-day, to which Marx and the socialist doctrines are quite unknown, the conviction that the war was in essence and in ultimate causation a capitalist war is firmly planted.

Trade routes, foreign markets, mining and railway concessions, coaling stations, access to and ownership of oil-wells, rubber plantations, tropical products and the labour to work them, colonies for profitable exploitation, the financing of foreign loans—the conduct of foreign relations was more and more absorbed in these great business "propositions." The dangerous nature of this economic competition, in which Governments were backing their own nationals, was manifested in the huge and growing armaments trades, themselves the ripest and most flourishing fruit of modern capitalism. War preparations were current capitalism, just as war itself was the supreme act or exploit of capitalism. "Signally it was a war of economics—of manufacture, equipment, of rival science, of social organization. It was a food war, a war of machinery, a chemical war, a war of fibres as of metals, a transport war, a war of petrol, a war of spare parts." [1] It was the revolt of machinery against its maker—the malign perversion of the science of industry from production to destruction that haunted the imagination of the inhabitants of Erewhon. Can the peoples that have witnessed the peaceful acts of mining, engineering, shipbuilding, chemicals and banking, the very pride and hope of modern capitalism, suddenly and simultaneously devoting themselves to slaughter and havoc, ever again recover the old confidence in their beneficent intentions? The thought will persistently recur, if the secret masters of these arts and instruments are able, from whatever gainful motive (for gain is their avowed motive), thus suddenly to turn them to our destruction, can we any longer sit or sleep or work under such a mastery?

To suspicious broodings on the origin of the war and shattering experience of its operation, reflections on the processes and products of the peace-making will make their due contribution. How coal and iron, the foundations of capitalism, overrode all "principles" of territorial settlement, how trade routes and commercial ports directed the carving of new Europe and the assignment of Asia to highly interested protectors or trustees, how war debts, indemnities, and the vast credit operations determine the prosperity or misery, the bondage or liberty, for generations to come, of all the peoples caught in the toils of war—when these hard facts stamp themselves, as they must, upon the minds of all informed citizens, and gradually permeate into the remote recesses of the popular intelligence, the result will be a great accession to the distrust of

[1] *The Economics of Peace*, by J. L. Garvin, p. 36.

"property" and the class-State which for several generations has been gathering consciousness in the working classes.

Some such analysis alone can furnish a reasonable answer to our initial question why the rulers of the Western States appeared to be so bent on stamping out Bolshevism that to this end they were willing, if necessary, to sacrifice a good peace and a pacific League of Nations.

Within each country the rulers, as representing the class-State, fear more a proletarian revolution which by physical force or economic pressure shall invade their property interests and break down their profitable control of industry, than they fear a bad settlement of international relations. A resumption of the war in its major meaning is not possible. The power of the enemy is broken and can be kept from recovery by the exercise of a moderate amount of military coercion. A Central and Eastern Europe kept in impotence with slow economic recovery and assisted into social order under a middle-class democracy, or even a screened autocracy, would be preferable to any settlement so secure as to draw away the thoughts and feelings of each nation from foreign affairs, in order to concentrate them upon problems of domestic reconstruction. For these governments and the classes that support them want a sufficiently unsettled world to justify the retention of moderate militarism, and they fear the interpretation which the newly roused desires and imaginations of their peoples put upon the processes of reconstruction.

In the United States, where the shorter duration of the war had not led the Government into irretrievable committals, a boldly precipitate abandonment of " reconstruction policy " was possible when the armistice came. But the British Government found itself so steeped in costly and alluring promises that no such extrication was feasible. Now, it may seem that this reconstruction policy contains nothing likely to imperil the existing order, and that it may be successful in its purpose of " buying off " the revolution. Education, housing, land settlement, public health, infant welfare, Whitley Councils, eight-hour days, statutory wage boards, represent an advance of social reform and capitalist concessions not ill adapted to this object. It is the offer of a substantial " bird in the hand " to a practical people. Will it succeed ? I think not, and for the following reasons. In the first place, the formulation of a Labour Programme, far outrunning this Reconstruction Programme and containing some definite challenges to property and business control which the ruling classes will not concede without a struggle, has won so wide an acceptance as to constitute a new stage in the social political thinking of the nation. It contains a plain demand for the socialization of a number of the most important and lucrative spheres of capitalist industry and for a new status for the workers in the operation of all public and private undertakings. It has crystallized the vague unrest which has prevailed during recent years into a new attitude of mind towards property and industry.

Secondly, the concrete actual advances in the organization both of capital and labour during the war preclude any return to the pre-war conditions. All hope or fear of effective competition has vanished over large fields of industry, combination reigns supreme in most of the great departments of extractive industry, manufacture, transport and finance. The pre-war habits of co-operat on and agreement, which modified competition in so many trades, have given place to a community of action which, though not yet represented in financial mergers, has gone too far for reversal. In business structure, Capitalism has advanced to what may be its final stage. The advance in the organization of labour though necessarily less complete (for dead capital admits of closer unity than live workmen), has been considerable. The power of the Triple Alliance is a new factor in the national situation. The net significance of these changes may be expressed by saying that they present clearly for the first time the alternatives of private or public monopoly in a number of the essential industrial services of the country. During the war several of these industries have been operated under schemes in which private ownership has been coupled with a joint control by the owners and the State, the latter intervening at various points in the supply of materials, fixation of costs in the several processes and of markets and selling prices, with taxation of excess profits. This method of attempting to reconcile the incentive of private profit with that of public service, a necessary and a useful compromise for the emergency of war-time, is by general consent ill-adapted to normal times. The patriotic efforts and sacrifices many able business men and workers were wil ing to make in war they will not make in peace, and the constant friction of State interference, tolerated with difficulty in war, would be intolerable in peace. Business men naturally ask the State to remove its hand and allow them to conduct their business in their own way with the old liberty of action.

But a return to the pre-war condition is impossible. For the measure of free competition which was even then a very poor protection for consumers against the practices of combination is in many cases so reduced that what these business men are really asking is the right to work the industry as a monopoly. There is no way of compelling persons to compete whose interests lead them to combine and who possess the means to make their combination effective.

In a word, the war has acted as a forcing process by which in a few years capitalism in these industries has virtually completed its evolution, passing out of the stage of competition into that of combination. Now, this change compels the nation to confront the issue between private profit and public service with a sharpness and immediacy that cannot be evaded. It is not possible to speculate with any confidence upon the early result of the conflict between the two principles. But I think that we may feel certain that in such fundamental industries as coalmining, railways, electricity, insurance and banking, the State, even under the existing play of political forces, will be impelled rapidly along the path of socialization in ownership if not in working. In certain other industries, possibly even in these, a halfway house will be found in State control of prices, or in other experiments designed to secure for the public service some fruits of the superior personal initiative and efficiency believed to inhere in private enterprise. It is exceedingly unlikely that any wholesale transformation of the fabric of industry will be attempted, or that any single solution for the new industrial problem will be found.

What concerns us here is first the fact that a

considerable section of the industrial system must certainly pass at an early date out of the sphere of private profiteering into that of public service, and that in another considerable section the State will seek to put strict limits upon profits. This, taken in conjunction with the new taxing policy which every modern State must now adopt for the "confiscation" of superfluous wealth in order to pay its war indebtedness and finance its new social policy, and with the expenses of the standard wage and employment insurance which each trade must bear, will have two important effects. A large proportion of the nation will be employed in the public service, and the great experiment of industrial democracy will be on its trial. If, as is often contended, it is not found possible to evolve a mode of public management which will maintain a fair standard of efficiency and discipline in these public services, while the employees in these services successfully extort by political pressure more than their proper share of the general wealth in wages, leisure and other conditions of employment, the failure will be manifest. For the scale upon which it will be tried could not enable its abuses to escape detection. It would not be possible to maintain large bodies of shirkers in the public services by subsidies drained from the employees in private enterprises. The experiment, therefore, must assume a directly moral character, viz. the discovery and application of incentives which shall feed the individual worker with a sense of social duty and shall enforce a discipline by methods the validity of which he shall freely recognize. It is precisely here that the "syndicalist" contribution should be available. For it may be easily admitted that existing governmental methods will not evoke sufficient sense of social service to run these industries with the desired efficiency. It is the problem of "bureaucracy" that has come up for solution. And democracy has a solution to offer, in the spiritual virtue of self-government. If democracy be government by public opinion, it will be effective in proportion as the opinion is that of an intimate and informed public. Such a public should be furnished in the workshops or other small business units in which whatever everybody does or neglects to do is known. It does not exist to-day in the voting ward of a modern city.

But does it follow that democracy is going to be allowed to realize itself in this or any other way?

Regarding the situation from the standpoint of evolution, it is too hastily assumed by socialists that the capitalist system is worked out and must yield to a system in which private profit shall give place to social service as the motive power. It is as yet by no means proven that wagedom is doomed, and that the new demands of workmen for industrial democracy cannot be resisted or compromised. Hitherto a fair amount of industrial peace has been purchasable by concessions which capital has been well able to afford. Is it certain that the resources of this policy are exhausted? It is curious that, amid all the thought and aspirations that go out towards the "labour international," so little attention should be given towards the possibility of a "capital international." Can it indeed be plausibly held that modern capitalism is worked out until that stage has been attained? Do not the sympathy of fear, communicated from the revolutionary countries to the more conservative, and the policy of mutual aid in resisting the revolutionary movement, concerted by the Western Governments, point to a wider and more stable plan of international capitalist co-operation by which the insurrection of the worker in the several countries may be checked or counteracted? A Holy Alliance of the older order, relying too visibly on armed power, might no longer prove a reliable instrument for the purpose. Capitalism, as a governing force, would need to work with a gloved hand in the world-rule which is contemplated by its master-minds, the chiefs of international commerce and finance. For one feature of our new world, made strikingly apparent by the war, is the fundamental importance of the relations between the developed and densely populated countries of the White West and the undeveloped countries upon which the former group depends for supplies of essential foods and raw materials. We have seen the importance of this relation in studying the causation of the war as contained in competing imperialism. But, just as within the nation competition of business has given place to combination, so with competition for empire. Once realize how the essence of empire is the power of economic exploitation, the policy of international capital becomes plain. It consists in concerted action (through a League of Nations or otherwise) to establish an economic peace by substituting a race cleavage for a class cleavage.

A few Western nations wield political and economic control over the vast areas of Africa and Asia which contain the chief supplies of vegetable and mineral oils, cotton, rubber and various other metals, foods and textile materials. The business firms favoured by these Powers, acting separately or in agreement, will be able to organize the required quantities of cheap submissive labour on the spot for the plantations, mines, and the collection and preparation of the exportable commodities. The railways and roads, the docks and shipping lines will be in their hands, together with the commercial and financial apparatus for exporting the tropical and other products to the home-countries, where bodies of well-paid, short-houred and contented Western workers, employees of the great combines, will by scientific manufacture transform them into serviceable shapes for consumption. If the hitherto untapped and uncultivated resources of Africa and Asia, South America and the Pacific Islands can be thus placed at the disposal of the business syndicates of the Western industrial countries, capitalism may be able to " square " labour in these countries, by making it a partner in a great sweating-system which will substitute the exploitation of foreign subject peoples for that of the Western working classes. If this is the way of securing property and winning industrial peace at home, the drive of combined political and economic forces will continually move more strongly in this direction. The underlying idea of substituting a racial for a class cleavage, and for bringing under the shelter of exploiting capitalism large favoured proletariats, perhaps to be transformed themselves into little shareholders, is not clearly developed even in the minds of the big financial and other business men whose plans are based upon the possibilities of such a profiteering future. It has not got to be a conscious clearly-thought-out design. Indeed, its execution would be hampered if its full shape and meaning were openly avowed. This was well illustrated by the rash conduct of the Empire Resources Development Committee early in the war in advertising its scheme for "imperializing" the land of our tropical dependencies and forcing native labour to grind out dividends for private syndicates and revenue for the Imperial Treasury. But this great new parasitism, by which the organized White peoples of the West exploit the coloured races and the backward countries for their private wealth and ease, may manifest itself as the natural drift of tendency for the imperialist nations in these troublous times.

In any case, a more thorough and effective development of the resources of these backward countries is certain to be set on foot, with capital and organizing personnel drawn from the centres of these Empires. These great importations of material and food will be essential to keep our home industries fully employed and our home populations satisfied. They cannot be bought by their full equivalent in export goods, for under what may be termed the natural operation of free exchange the prices of raw materials and food-stuffs would for a long time to come remain on a higher level than the prices of manufactured export goods. Thus there will be the strongest possible inducements for business syndicates, developing and controlling the foreign supplies, to organize the labour and other costs of production on "cheap" terms, i.e. to employ forced or sweated labour and to use Governmental aids to obtain concessions of land and other business opportunities at small cost to them. Much, therefore, of these tropical and other overseas products will come in to the Western countries as rents of monopoly or high profits on low-paid native labour. A portion of this surplus gain can be utilized to support a relatively high level of comfort for the Western working classes, who will insist upon higher real wages, shorter hours, adequate provision against unemployment, ill-health, old age and other emergencies. The workers would take their share partly in high money-wages, partly in low prices for imported products, partly in social services rendered by a State which drew a large tax-revenue from leasing "Crown lands" in the colonies and protectorates to licensed business syndicates, and from taxation of the high incomes derived from this exploitation. By such political-economic policy it might be possible for the capitalist classes in the West to buy industrial peace at home. We doubt if any other means of making the necessary concessions to "the claims of labour" without endangering their mastery is available. This, we think, is the great temptation to which the organized workers of the West are exposed: the offer to come into a limited international, under which both capital and labour in an oligarchy of great nations shall "live upon" the rich natural resources and the subject peoples of the backward and the undeveloped countries. An oligarchic League of Nations, exercising protectorate and mandatory powers over the greater portion of the weaker peoples, can make this great extension of capitalism under the guise of pacific settlement, trusteeship of "derelict empires" and the organization of the latent resources of countries declared to be incapable of political and economic self-government.

A group of Western capitalistic governments, calling themselves a League of Nations, or the Great Powers, or the Civilized World, might by such a policy achieve several valuable objects. They might: (1) establish a lucrative monopoly of essential supplies of foods and materials for private gain; (2) strengthen their hold upon their respective national governments by making them participants in the exploitation of the subject areas, thus reducing the burden of taxation which otherwise might fall upon their shoulders; (3) by substituting cheap and manageable native force for the expensive and unreliable armies of White conscripts maintain order abroad and at home; and (4) keep their own home workers in ease, comfort and contentment, by making them small shareholders in this exploitation of their weaker brethren. Whether the organized workers of the so-called Western democracies will have the humanity, justice, foresight and courage needed to resist this temptation may be the test issue of the near future.

CHAPTER II

THE LIBERATION OF LABOUR

WE have seen that the common case for Bolshevism, Syndicalism, Guild Socialism, Industrial Unionism rests upon three assumptions, first that economic issues must play an ever-increasing part in politics; secondly, that economic justice and security for the workers can only be got by a proletarian control of Government; thirdly, that such proletarian Government is only possible by the substitution of functional for regional representation. So long as these assumptions appear to the common intelligence in substance valid, the struggle to overthrow "the Capitalist State" and to destroy its economic supports will continue with increasing bitterness. Their validity is not successfully impugned by insisting that the interests of consumers ought to prevail over the interests of producers, that in this demand for proletarian domination the interests of the consumers are wrongly ignored, and that the existing institutions of political democracy are necessary to protect the consumer. This theory of our economic life misrepresents the operative facts and forces of existing society. For it is only in a formal sense that consumption of wealth can be represented as the end or aim of economic processes. The productive processes of industry absorb nearly all the time, energy, thought and continuous interest of the great majority of men and women. Consumption, though of more immediate vital significance, occupies a subordinate place in consciousness. Moreover, man as worker is closely associated with his fellow-man, as consumer is a detached unit. The politics of the workshop have, therefore, a reality and a social meaning far superior to the politics of the citizen-consumer. It is, then, no adequate reply to the syndicalist "idea" to point to the necessity of maintaining the present basis of the State in the interest of the consumer. The worker knows how feeble an instrument it is for such an end, and if it were a better instrument, he could not concede its sovereignty in the economic sphere. Ought we then to capitulate to the syndicalist idea? By no means, unless we accept as final the first of the three assumptions above cited, upon which the others rest, viz. that economic issues must play an increasing and a dominant part in politics. And by this assumption is signified, not merely that the State must take on a larger number of definitely economic functions, but that the economic functions of the State must continually absorb a larger share of the interests and activities which form the staple of politics. So long as the activities connected with the acquisition of economic values bulk so largely as they do in the conscious interest of men, the pressure of producers' dominance in the working of the State and the struggle for the defence of "vested interests" and industrial mastery will continue. Proletarian organized force will be met by capitalistic organized force, political, intellectual and in the last resort physical. The amiable notion that education and publicity of information will serve to restore social peace, by winning the acceptance of a theory of the economic harmony between capital and labour, a restoration and humane remodelling of the Bastiat doctrine, is quite chimerical. Plausible as this doctrine of economic harmony was in a world of "free" competition, it is quite unmeaning in a world of combination. Education and publicity will only serve to sharpen the sense of economic injustice and conflicting interests in a world where the limited necessaries and conveniences of life are distributed so largely by force, cunning, chance and favour.

There is, however, an escape from the apparent impasse. It consists in a rapid and early liberation of mankind from the tyranny, not of wagedom nor of capitalism, though this liberation follows, but of industrialism itself. If we can be members of a human society which gives less and less of its total fund of time, energy, thought and feeling to those tasks of production which we call industrial, a society in which economic values, and the property and industry on which they hinge, play a diminishing part in personal and social life, we shall escape what appears otherwise to be the long and devastating struggle between the forces of proletarian attack and capitalist defence. Several tendencies contribute to make such a liberation possible. There are many signs that we are entering a new era of industrial revolution which in a single generation may raise the productivity of human labour to so high a level as to enable any decently ordered society to secure the material necessaries and comforts for all its members without imposing painful toil on anyone.[1] The clear perception that social peace is only possible upon such terms immensely stimulates the transformation of the industrial system under the new scientific impulse. The age of steam has passed. We are entering on the age of electricity : the sciences of physics and chemistry are yielding every year new fruits of knowledge which feed thousands of trained and watchful inventors and adapters with ideas for improvement of machinery and processes, for utilization of waste products, or for other economies in handling the resources of nature. Not only is this growth of the applied sciences intensive, it is extensive : and the spread of education brings innumerable minds into closer contact and co-operation, thus providing an accelerated pace in scientific progress. Not less important, the neglect and contempt of science by the practical man, nowhere more manifest than in this country, are yielding to a more intelligent utilitarianism. The new place of prominence assumed by engineering and chemical industries is forcing the claims of

[1] Take, for example, the new possibilities of food-supplies which cheapening processes of the fixation of nitrogen open up, or the estimated saving of fuel obtainable by the electrification of British railways (computed to amount to 150 million tons per annum). By the use of the Wincott Furnace Sir Robert Hadfield claims to have reduced the quantity of coal required for heating one ton of steel from 15 cwt. to 2. By the Still Engine (combined steam and gas or oil) additional effective work done equals " 29 per cent. when the steam portion is operated non-condensing, and 40 per cent. when operated condensing."

" The scientist has this to say to the world to-day. If you insist on going to war again, the power which I shall give you will only enable you more effectively to destroy the world. But if you will remain at peace and accept the help I have to offer, it will lead you to such wealth as you have not imagined."—Lord Moulton, *Observer*, June 22, 1919.

scientific research and analysis on every industry and bringing home the uses of exact measurement, the foundation of all economy. The same spirit of order and exactitude is engaged in the art of business administration, bringing live intelligence to bear upon every act in every process by which material is converted into product, and preventing human arrangement from sinking into hard mechanical routine. All these advances are reflected and registered in improved bookkeeping and accountancy, and in the wider art of business finance with which the critical processes of buying and of selling are closely associated. A greater faith in progress, and in knowledge as the instrument of progress, is penetrating even to the more backward trades. This new technique and modern art of business administration have never yet been free to express their full potency in actual production. Almost everywhere they have been held up and restrained by the failure of markets to afford an adequate response to their increased productivity. This persistent check upon full sustained production in the most developed industries was responsible for two conspicuous forms of waste, the unemployment of recurring periods of trade depression and the absorption of large quantities of potentially productive energy in the wasteful processes of competition for markets. The substitution of combination for competition does not provide a remedy for the waste. The check upon production through failure of adequately expanding markets still operates. But it takes shape in an ordered "regulation of output." Every business man has long been aware that in all the developed industries production has been straining against the barrier of limited markets. The new technique of the electric age, with its vast powers of output, cannot be realized so long as this limitation of market continues. It appears impossible to reap these great economies of production under a system of private enterprise for profit. For it is the apparent impossibility of marketing at a profit the full product of the industry that has been crabbing the pace of industrial progress.

How can this liberation be achieved? War experience helps us to find an answer. For several years the normal position was reversed. Instead of sellers importuning buyers, buyers were importuning sellers. The effective demand of would-be consumers everywhere kept stimulating producers to their utmost efforts. The productive energies of our civil population were strained to the utmost intensity, all the waste competitive labour was squeezed out of the distributive trades, and every sort of improvised economy of tools, labour and materials was employed to meet the demand of the market. I need not dwell upon the quite evident causes of this reversal of the ordinary relations between supply and demand, the shortage of supplies of labour and materials due to military operations, on the one hand, and, on the other, the increased demand due to the immense public expenditure upon supplies for the forces and the increased private expenditure of the great mass of working-class families whose incomes were improved by war conditions.

The economic lesson is unmistakable. Artificially stimulated consumption of goods called into play reserve powers of production which, contrary to all expectation, were able to maintain the people of this country during the first three years of the war upon a considerably higher general level of material comfort than at any previous time. Even if we make some allowance for American subsidies of food, paid for by selling securities, the exhibition of reserve productivity within our national economic system is remarkable.[1] It was, of course, accompanied by certain heavy human strains of overtime and speeding up, of encroachment on the leisure of the young and old, and other injuries of the emergency. But can any careful observer doubt that it warrants the belief that any reasonably effective organization of our existing technique and economic resources before the war would have enabled us as a nation to turn out double the amount of wealth we were actually turning out, without any excessive tax upon the human energies of our people? If to such testimony we add the reasonable expectations of the new technique, the new art of administration and the new finance, may it not seem possible, or even likely, that within the next few years our productive powers will be adequate, if fully utilized, to supply all the ordinary wants of our population, with a constantly diminishing call upon their working time and energy? But an indispensable condition of this productivity will be the high consumption of goods and leisure by our people. Increased productivity and improved distribution are thus indissolubly bound together in the reformation of industry.

[1] Moreover, very little of these subsidies was contributory to our own resources; almost the whole was absorbed in contributions to the fighting and consumptive resources of our Allies.

The logic of the movement in which these various processes merge is this. Industrial service is not and cannot be made interesting and pleasurable in itself to most of those engaged in it. Hitherto this absence of inherent attraction has been compensated by appeals to competitive greed in the capitalists and managers, and to the necessity of earning a living in the proletarian employees. The play of these individual incentives is no longer adequate to the support of these industries. It is necessary to convert them into services that are social, not only in their results, but in the conscious operation of their processes. The consciousness of men that they are "working for society" may not go far as a positive incentive to industry and efficiency in the performance of essentially dull and disagreeable work. Nay, there is abundant evidence to support the judgment that work done for the State or the municipality is slower and slacker than the same sort of work done for a private employer. Upon this citation of "the Government Stroke" the case against Socialism takes its chief stand. The full force of this case, however, rests upon the assumption that all the conditions of employment except the personality of the employer remain the same in a socialized industry. It assumes a direct bureaucratic management. But the assumption is inapplicable to the new Socialism, which severs ownership from operation, and entrusts the latter function to a body mainly constituted of the different grades of workers in the industry. This situation would materially affect their feelings towards their work, would introduce a new element of free will into its performance. Moreover, any present comparison between the efficiency of work under private and public enterprise must take into account the new resentment against profiteering. This trade sentiment is admittedly responsible in mining and in other essential industries for a dangerous reduction of output, which to a large degree invalidates those past comparisons between the product of labour in public and private enterprise on which defenders of private capitalism rely.

Still more important, however, will be the effect of the large reduction of the work-day which the new technique and organization of industry will make practicable. For in essentially dull industry it is not the first step but the last which costs. A reduction of eight hours to six reduces the human cost by far more than a quarter, provided it is not accompanied by an intensification of effort. A limited amount of regular work, of a socially useful kind, done as a matter of duty by every able-bodied citizen as his proper contribution to the social fund from which each family draws its ordinary supply of the necessaries and conveniences of life, would be accepted as equitable, and would not be felt to be oppressive to human personality in its performance. It might soon come to be regarded as a "social exercise," an extension and a social utilization of the physical exercises, equally dull and unpleasant in themselves, which so many members of the leisured or sedentary classes voluntarily undertake for hygienic purposes.

Such industrial work can never be made interesting and pleasurable to its performers, but it can be made tolerable and of willing acceptance, provided that it is light and equal in its incidence and that its product is recognized to be apportioned equitably. It is towards a solution of the industrial problem on these lines that we are groping our way through Whitley Councils, Trade Boards, Syndicalism, Guilds, Nationalization and State Controls. The apparent object of these fumbling experiments is to heal industrial strife and get the ordinary work of the world done upon the new combinatory basis. But the real object is to rescue humanity from the thraldom of mechanical industry, by reducing the pressure which industry has hitherto exercised on life. There is no need for a class of industrial serfs in any modern society. Properly organized and apportioned, industry should fall lightly on the life of our people. Its efforts and its conflicts should pass, so to speak, into the subconsciousness of modern society. The control over the powers of nature and of human organization which now exist make this liberation feasible. Only by such liberation is industrial peace attainable. It does not imply the absorption of all economic activities under State Socialism or any variant of Socialism. The trouble has lain predominantly in two classes of industry.

First come the great highly organized capitalistic trades engaged in producing or distributing the routine goods and services which are the chief necessaries of life for all members of the community. This class includes the staple manufactures and the chief agencies for transport, distribution and finance. The second class contains the backward and sweated industries, mostly parasites eking out a precarious life by utilizing feeble or derelict labour for squeezing out precarious profits in low business organizations. The new public policy is engaged, partly in forcing these industries into more highly organized forms, partly in stamping them out. Social ownership is essential for the first class. It is no longer safe or possible to leave society at the mercy of profiteering combines, wrangling with their employees for their respective shares of the loot got from the consumer. Status, the standard minimum and the destruction of profiteering can only be compassed by socialization of this type of industry. For lower types of industry public control of conditions of employment and of prices may well suffice. For some of these lower types shade off insensibly into the economic activities of arts and crafts, distinguished from the routine industries by retaining considerable elements of interest, skill and freedom for the individual worker in them. To this type may belong not only the bulk of the smaller skilled handicrafts and many personal services, but large sections of agriculture in the hands of free peasant occupiers. Whenever the element of personal interest and pleasure inheres in any productive work, it is wrong for organized society to interfere with the free service which such labour can yield. The fact that profit may be a considerable motive in the performance of this work does not warrant us in placing such restraints upon its performance as will hamper the freedom and impair the personal interest of the worker.

For the main object in liberating man from the heavy chains of mechanical industry is not to make him idle, but so to reduce the pressure of uninteresting and disagreeable employment as to give increased facilities for interesting and agreeable employment. William Morris's poetical sketch of a society where all necessary productive work is so interesting on its own account that no reward of ownership is required is manifestly unattainable. But civilization should mean a diminishing proportion of dull and oppressive industry and an increasing freedom for self-chosen occupations. It is a chief end of science to conduce to this progressive liberation of man. But the achievement of this requires that science itself be rescued from subservience to property and power and be placed at the service of man. While a portion of the new liberty thus conferred would pass from oppressive modes of industry into the freedom of pleasurable production, an increasing share would go to the satisfaction of those activities and interests which lie outside the economic sphere. Friendship, family life, knowledge, recreation, travel, citizenship, the cultivation of unexplored riches of personality, all await this economic deliverance. Those who would impede it with the panic cries of confiscation, anarchy and Bolshevism are enemies of the human race. It is true that such a deliverance will heavily impair the rights of property and the class control of industry which have hitherto prevailed. But with the changes in economic structure and in human valuations these rights and this control are no longer tolerable. Property is a permanently valuable institution. It must be the right of every human being to have secured to him for his sole personal use and enjoyment his "proper" share of the wealth produced by social co-operation and the bounty of nature. But property must be shorn of industrial control, that is to say, it must no longer be an instrument of profit. The materials and tools of routine industry must be social property. Under such reformed industrial structure property will be endowed with a vast increase of human value, for the wastes of excess and of deficiency, due to its present maldistribution and oppressive uses, will be eliminated. But when profiteering is removed from industry, the total pressure of property and of industry upon human life will be lightened. Economics will be the servant, not the master, of humanity.

This brings me back by a somewhat circuitous route to a refutation of the purely occupational or functional conception of representative government which we found to be the root-idea of the movement. It rests on the assumption that the earning of a livelihood by productive work is and must remain the predominant activity of man and that association for this purpose, therefore, furnishes the strongest basis of common interest. The process of economic reform, as I interpret it, furnishes a contradiction of this assumption. It indicates how social control of the new industrial technique will so cheapen the ordinary goods and services in terms of human cost as in effect to communalize them. His ordinary share in necessary forms of wealth thus secured to everybody, as a matter of course and in return for a light normal contribution of routine service on his part, such industry and the property associated with it will become relatively unimportant factors in the fuller human life which increased leisure and enlarged opportunity will place at everybody's disposal. In other words, the free or non-industrial side of life will assert its predominance, and the unity of neighbourhood will prevail over that of the workshop as the groundwork of social co-operation in politics. While, therefore, it may be reasonably claimed that, so long as economic issues continue to bulk so largely in current politics as they do now, economic function has a rightful claim to be represented in the structure of democracy, there is no warrant for allowing it to displace the accepted local basis of representation or to assert a supremacy which is opposed to the true trend of social evolution in what has been termed the "neo-technic age."

CHAPTER III

REVOLUTION BY CONSENT

I HAVE sketched a plan of political industrial evolution by which it seems reasonably possible that a people like the British, escaping the destructive experience of a class-war, might attain a form of moderate socialist-communism compatible not merely with a high measure of personal freedom but with private enterprise in many fields of economic activity. But the feasibility of this process turns upon the acceptance and application of a radically new conception of the functions of property and industry in a modern society. This acceptance and application may conceivably be achieved by moral and intellectual pressure on the propertied and ruling classes, accompanied by an undermining of their political and economic strength through the combined action of the ballot-box and industrial force. Much, perhaps all, so far as the next era of our history is concerned, will depend upon the relative importance of the part played in this process by persuasion and force, whether that force be constitutionally exercised or not. For unless property and capitalist rule in industry can be transformed by a process of consent to which the holders are in some sense willing parties, the whole process is likely to be held up for a generation or more, the interval occupied in an embittered and a devastating class war. For the issue, as I see it, is not between a proletarian domination secured by revolutionary violence and one secured by the successful combination of the vote and strike. I do not believe that either physical or constitutional force is adequate to secure success. Against the former the power of our organized State would be more than sufficient even under a Labour Government. A revolution by constitutional force only seems more feasible so long as the actual power of property over politics and public opinion is not adequately realized. When we realize how powerful is the hold of property upon the Press, the schools, the pulpit, the platform, the public-house, the music-hall, the "pictures," we understand how impregnable it is against assault from without. Unless an entirely new "psychology of the people" is produced or revealed as the result of the war strains and infections, no labour or socialist party, figuring as political democracy, will have sufficient solidarity, concentration of purpose and numerical strength to bring about a constitutional revolution. A strong wedge of organized labour might, by strikes and other shock-tactics, extort from employers and from a capitalist Government solid concessions, compensated by losses either for unorganized labour in their own country or, perhaps, in accordance with the policy of imperialist exploitation I have sketched, for subject labour in backward countries. But there are no signs of such solidarity of working-class interests and purposes in Britain, in America or France as to prefigure a revolutionary electorate imposing and maintaining a proletarian government capable of enforcing a swift and complete transformation of the institution of property and the control of industry. The defences of the interestocracy against a policy of constitutional or unconstitutional violence are far too strong. If any such transformation is to be brought about, it must be accompanied by so wide and deep a measure of consent among the propertied classes and their social supporters as will paralyse or weaken their defences. In other words, a British revolution can only be made good by an appeal to reason and justice. It cannot be made except by detaching large sections of what may be termed the natural allies of conservatism. This sounds a hard saying to socialist and other proletarian parties confident in their force and numbers to enable them to impose their will and reconstitute society. The idea of force as a remedy is with them usually glossed by the sense that they are the majority and that social justice is contained in the will of the majority. Others, of course, ignoring all appeals to the liberal concepts of a bourgeois morality, read all history as movement of a class war in which the conquering will is always that of a conscious minority imposing terms not only on the enemy, but upon its own less conscious following.[1] The dramatization of force as remedy, and the spurious moral endorsement it has received in the Great War, will have made the appeal to reason everywhere more difficult. That is the greatest of all moral costs of the war.

To spirits still throbbing with the war passion, how convincing the logic of Syndicalism sounds! "You cannot smash the Capitalist by political

[1] For a trenchant application of this definitely Marxist doctrine to British conditions see *Creative Revolution*, by Eden and Cedar Paul (Allen and Unwin).

weapons, because, as things now are, he can always contrive to get those weapons into his own hands and use them for squashing you. The one weapon he cannot steal is the Strike. With your votes the Capitalist can play tricks. He can capture them, he can manipulate them, he can persuade you to give them to him in promises which he keeps in the letter but violates in the spirit. But the Strike is a direct blow which he cannot evade, and which if repeated often enough, is certain in the long run to knock him out." [1] So it is very difficult at such a moment to ask proletarian revolutionists to turn their attention to converting their enemies instead of destroying them. To their impatience the very notion that such conversion is possible appears absurd and is suspected as a wile of defence. "The powerful classes who own riches and wield industrial sway, the great ones of the earth, have got their property and power by force and will only yield them to superior force. Christian Socialists and Social reformers of their own order have often appealed to them in the name of justice and humanity to convert their ownership into public trusts and their personal leadership to social service. Nothing comes of these appeals but the flabby philanthropy of some profit-sharing or copartnership. The strong set interests, incapable of seeing either the injustice or the inhumanity of the economic system they control, will only listen to and understand force. They have evolved a set of intellectual and moral defences of their own, an economic theory and a political philosophy which provide what spiritual supports they need. Indeed, these class-dogmas they widely use as propaganda for breaking the

[1] Dr. J. E. Jacks, *Observer*, April 27, 1919.

solidarity of the working-class movement. Why, therefore, should we listen to your proposal to win the 'consent' of conservative interests or conceive it possible to undermine and weaken their defences?"

My answer is that underneath this as every other issue of tactics lies an issue of principle. I am not with the moral absolutionists who would cast away all carnal weapons, trusting to the sword of the spirit. Recognizing that every use of force weakens the appeal of reason and justice, I nevertheless hold that in every act of human conduct some alloy of force is necessary to a sound economy of achievement. I even doubt if any act of persuasion, education or conversion is unaccompanied by some element of pressure which in the last resort partakes of physical compulsion. In collective action of every kind such force does and must exist. Though for convenience of thought a sharp antithesis exists between physical compulsion and reasonable will, it cannot be treated as absolute and ultimate. In the last resort believers in any reasonable order of the universe must hold that no display of physical force is utterly blind, but that it carries, in however clumsy and wasteful a fashion, an element of direction to which a purposive or rational significance must be given. But though this reconciling view deserves recognition, it need not be carried so far as to "rationalize" or "moralize" the use of force as if it were a wholly reliable play of blind purpose. On the contrary, all history exhibits progress in terms of the subjection of force to reason So even in the more v olent collective operation of mass humanity we find reason playing a continually larger part. Though realistic analysis of the French Revolution tends to depreciate the direct part of the rhetorical formulas as operative motives, none can deny that they were necessary for generating a revolutionary energy composed in no small measure of their moral and intellectual meaning. Recent revolutions, though definitely war products, are loaded, sometimes overloaded, with instruments of rational persuasion.

In a word, the revolutionary spirit or movement must contain both ingredients, and it is a question of composition and proportion. It is easily admitted that "ideals," i.e. the spiritual and intellectual appeals, are necessary in order to fire and to sustain the enthusiasm of the revolutionaries. Even among our people, though far less susceptible by temperament to such appeals, these rational and emotional elements must be fused with the cruder appeals to use physical or political force for gain and power. But the explosion of these reasonable "bombs" among the enemy for purposes of spiritual conversion is a tactic whose value it is more difficult to appreciate. I have approached its advocacy by dwelling upon the otherwise impenetrable strength of the class defences. And to this point I here revert. There is no ground for believing that an effective transformation of our social economic system can be achieved by any available muster of proletarian force, unaccompanied by some such organized endeavour to convert, detach and win over considerable numbers of the present allies of reaction. Proletarian force, unaccompanied by an appeal to reason, will consolidate resistance.

Democracy with economic justice cannot be got by any mere display of political and economic force. The threat of physical coercion, either by armed violence or by the direct action of a general strike, paralyses all the latent liberalism in the classes and welds them into a stiff, unyielding body, using for their successful defence the better equipped forces which wealth, prestige and superior generalship place at their disposal. The notion that the mercenary forces of reaction will desert their paymasters in obedience to the proletarian appeal is only valid when discipline and loyalty are undermined by intolerable grievances of service. No doctrine is more fatal to social revolution than that which presents the achievement of proletarian domination as the inevitable outcome of an evolutionary process in which class interests, operating as forces, are the only real historical factors. For the effect of this "scientific" determinism is to remove from the peoples the moral and intellectual means of salvation. The real hope for democracy lies not in a barren "must" but in a must with an "ought" behind it. Unless the peoples make good their appeal to the reason and justice of this "ought" they cannot generate among themselves the will to organize and press to victory. Even their physical force and strength of numbers will crumble in their hands, if it is not held together by a sense of the justice and reason of their cause. We have seen how necessary this intellectual and moral idealism was as a generator of national war-energy. In our people no cold dogmas of evolutionary determinism can take its place. They must see right and reason in their cause. But, more important still, they must apply these resources to break the confidence of their "enemy" in the justice of his cause. To neglect to use these instruments of spiritual conversion would be fatal folly. It is not true that the fortresses of property and privilege will only yield to proletarian force. They will not so yield, and their resistance will be successful. Such concessions as may be wrung by such sudden force will be won back or compensated by other unseen encroachments. Only by using the sword of the spirit to wound and weaken the self-confidence of the garrison can the citadel be captured. It may not be easy to persuade the fighting unit that the goodness of their cause is a stronger weapon than the violence of numbers, and that sound strategy will rely more upon moral propaganda than on strikes or votes. They will be disposed to suspect such pleas as enervating devices to choke off "the revolution." And there is a school of pacifists whose reliance upon moral force is so absolute as to warrant this interpretation. This absolutist logic compels them to reject all action, not merely by physical force but by the sheer force of majority domination as a weakening of the power of moral government. This logic I hold to be unsound in overstressing the opposition between moral and physical and in repudiating the harmonious co-operation of the two as a degrading compromise. To treat human beings as if their nature were purely spiritual and would be moved by spiritual motives alone is to falsify the actual facts of life. An alloy of lower motives will continue to be needed in every department of human conduct : moral progress is measured in terms of the weakening of the alloy.

The grosser forms of the will-to-power will and must play their part in the proletarian revolution. But no revolution will succeed unless these forces are subordinate to the arts of peaceable persuasion. The hard-shell convictions of the sanctity and immutability of the existing institutions of property and economic rule have already been shaken among many members of the possessing classes and their social allies. This is not merely a policy of concessions and sacrifice inspired by fear. It is also the voice of humanity and justice reaching the conscience and the reason through the wrappings of interest and custom. To further this liberation of ideas and sentiments in the more sensitive and mobile minds of the possessing and ruling classes should be a primary consideration in the tactics of the revolution. Every excess, every manifest injustice and cruelty in the pressure of the proletarian movement, every unfair discrimination, hardens their hearts and closes their intellect to the just claims of the people. There are whole groups among our "educated" classes, hitherto the intellectual and social supporters of the stiff rights of property, whose willing allegiance is now wavering and shaken. Many teachers, clergy, *littérateurs*, lawyers, journalists, artists, are deeply touched by the ideal of a juster and better social order. Even more significant is the new attitude of the scattering of business men, financiers, railroad men, manufacturers, who, brushing aside the policy of emollients and concessions, declare boldly for a reconstruction of industry under the joint control of brain and hand workers and consumers, operating as a public service. The test issue is one of psychology and ethics. It is commonly misrepresented as an attempt suddenly to eliminate selfish interest as an economic motive and to substitute a sentiment of social welfare. It may be taken for granted that industrial reconstruction in this country will not proceed on the lines of this wholesale conversion. Its immediate objectives, viz. sound conditions of work and life for all producers, the elimination of private profit as an economic motive, and a voice in management, demand not merely the retention but the enhancement of such personal interests as are required to evoke the best individual contributions to production. Security of livelihood, of leisure and of other opportunities is the first condition of an efficient working life. Upon it may be grafted all sorts of personal ambitions which will act as incentives to higher economic efficiency. The insecurity of livelihood and of any standard of life hitherto prevailing has damaged these incentives. Nor is it true that in the administration of the fundamental industries the hope and opportunity of immense and incalculable profit are necessary to evoke the highest qualities of judgment and initiative. In such industries, even under the existing system, very little of the profit goes to reward the managers, inventors, scientific or business experts, who give out these productive services. Most profit goes as an unearned gratuity to the shareholders for the supply of capital which was in most cases obtainable at the ordinary market rate. When we add that much profit comes from one or other of three anti-social sources, viz. the under-remuneration of labour, the overcharging of consumers and the ousting of competitors from their market, we recognize how flimsy is the claim that private profit is a necessary guarantee for the conduct of a socially efficient business. Profit, as at present made and apportioned, involves a great waste of economic incentive. Whatever is required in the way of special personal gain, as an addition to the standard wage or salary, can be provided far better under a service from which the gratuitous, hazardous and excessive payment of profit is removed. Well regulated industry will rely upon measured incentives, applied in all departments of hand and brain work to supplement the normal payments, when experience shows that such supplements are needed to evoke the best efforts. The notion that a proletarian government of industry would assume every man to be animated by so strong a sense of public duty that he can be relied upon to do his best upon a fixed secure salary is a wholly unwarrantable assumption. The elimination of private profit does not imply an exclusive reliance upon a sense of public duty as the economic motive: it replaces a wasteful by an economical application of such personal incentives. If to some revolutionary enthusiasts this retention of personal material incentives seems to be a betrayal of the ideal of absolute economic equality, my reply is that a British proletarian revolution will make this compromise precisely for the same reason that it will make the compromise between the use of physical and moral force to bring about the revolution. Just as its conduct of the revolution will be based upon a "common-sense" recognition of the duality of human nature, so in the working of the new economic order there will be no attempt to exaggerate the strength of the direct appeal of social welfare to the average sensual man. It will be recognized that much useful work will be dull, hard and distasteful, and that reliance on the "dignity of labour" in the service of society will not suffice to get it done. So, likewise, it will be recognized that some of the higher inventive, administrative and artistic qualities, fraught with immense public gain, are found in men who are not content to work for glory but insist upon material rewards. These considerations will enforce a compromise with idealism which may be distasteful to some reformers. But when it is perceived that in this way the uncompromising opposition of the possessing classes can be broken, and a transformation of the social economic system be attained with a minimum of violence and the best assurance of lasting success, the curious genius of the British people for choosing the line of least resistance will lead them to take this path.

PART V

A NEW WORLD

CHAPTER I

CHANGES OF NATIONAL STATUS

FEW facts are "hard" in the sense that they are certain, the same for all men, and enduring. It is important to bear this in mind in any attempt to describe what the war has done to the world. For some of those changes which stand out most conspicuously as results of the war and seem to have a determinant bearing upon the world's future may turn out to be of quite transient importance. This is particularly applicable to many of the damages of war that bulk so big in their immediate significance to-day. The self-healing powers of nature in every department of organic life are a wonderful testimony to creative purpose. This will find its clearest expression in a stimulation of the reproductive powers of man in areas where the loss of population by war, famine, pestilence or migration has been most marked. The prudential restraints operative in all more civilized countries will doubtless moderate, but will not cancel, this natural process of recovery. Thus will the hardest of all facts of war, the destruction of human life, be softened.

The processes of economic recuperation in devastated and impoverished countries are quickened by like natural responses to the urgency of human needs. All recent history attests the rapidity of this recuperation. And forces are now available which, if allowed free play, can immensely accelerate recovery from the economic wounds of war. For productivity is now recognized to depend to a diminishing extent upon labour and embodied capital, and to an increasing extent upon ideas, applied through technology and organization. But, as we have seen, this fruitful application of ideas through reliable co-operation of the minds and bodies of men depends upon good will, making the economic likewise the moral problem.

Will these recuperative powers of nature, reinforced and directed by reason and good will, get free operation in this new war-made world? Every sort of handicap seems to be imposed. The war-spirit seems to have struck back at those very healing forces and to have done its utmost to paralyse their action.

The political changes brought about by the war carry the instability and weakness of their origin. New self-governing States, Poland, Czecho-Slovakia, Jugo-Slavia, liberated not by their own efforts but by foreign force and enlarged with unassimilable alien populations, are at once the prey of internal dissensions and of external hostilities. Launched on an imperialist career by their own reckless ambitions or the militarist designs of the great conquering Powers, they remain a danger to themselves and to their neighbours. All the other conquerors have made large incorporations of alien holdings on their own account by annexation, protectorate or mandatory power. Thus, in a war for liberty, the total area of imperialism and subject nationalities has been appreciably increased. For, apart from the transfer of subject peoples from the conquered to the conquering Powers, many millions of Germans, Austrians, Hungarians and Turks, and the lands they owned and occupied, have been handed over to their enemies as spoils of war: France has finally absorbed Morocco into her colonial system, our new authority in Persia does not differ in any considerable measure from that of a Protectorate, while Japan has extended her real area of control in China far beyond the territory held by Germany.

Not only is a larger portion of the world held by force in imperial subjection, but the destruction of the German and Turkish Empires and the appropriation of these territories by Britain, France and Italy have diminished the number of the great Empires. Finally, the share of Britain in this distribution of the spoils is of such magnitude as largely to increase the actual and the proportionate size of our Empire in the world. For there exists no immediate power in any Council of the League of Nations to distinguish any of the mandatory areas we hold from our Protectorates. If the British Empire was already before the war too big, widespread and various for effective imperial control, and an object of jealousy and suspicion to other Powers, these defects and dangers are now greater. Many of the tropical products of which the whole world is in need now lie exclusively within our political control. Hitherto the substantial equality of commercial opportunities given to foreign merchants by our Free Trade system has turned the edge of enmity. But the new policy of preference and imperial conservation, if continued and developed, could not long escape challenge from Powers whose requirements for industry and consumption are identical with ours and who find themselves at a disadvantage by reason of our monopoly of tropical supplies. Nor is it merely or mainly a question of trade. The economic value of empire to the imperialist interests lies more and more in the gains of the financial ownership and exploitation of the mines, railways and plantations, and the native labour available on easy terms upon the spot. Whatever formal equality of opportunity be accorded, foreign capitalists and concessionaires are well aware that they can only participate indirectly and to a small extent in the more lucrative business propositions.

The large extension of British, and in less measure of French and Italian empire, especially in Africa, is, therefore, a new factor of considerable significance in the political-economic situation.

Of more immediate importance is the direct shift in the economic and financial strength of nations brought about by the war. At the outbreak of war the position of the leading nations of the world, as indicated by their estimated wealth per head of population,[1] was as follows. The United States led by a long way, with £424. Next came Argentina with £340. The United Kingdom and Australia came third with £318, followed in order by France (£303), Canada (£300) and Germany (£244). Russia came lowest of the European countries with £85, and Japan stood far lowest on the whole list with £44.

Though no statistics of the post-war position are yet available, the principal alterations are no

[1] J. C. Stamp, "The Wealth and Income of the Chief Powers," *Journal of the Statistical Society*, July 1919.

matter of dispute. In present wealth only two of the belligerents have been large gainers—the United States and Japan. Among the neutrals, Argentina will rank easily first, by virtue of the enhanced profits of her food exports. Canada and Australia will have risen both positively and proportionately in the scale of wealth, notwithstanding their large war expenditure. Holland, the Scandinavian countries and Spain will also have improved their position. Switzerland's position will not materially have altered. The victorious Allies will have suffered in different measures, the United Kingdom least, while Germany, Austria and Russia will stand for available present wealth at the bottom of the list.

All estimates of present wealth and of future powers of recuperation are, of course, impaired by considerations of war debt and indemnities. Though for such estimates internal indebtedness does not count, the heavy obligations to foreign lenders incurred by France, Italy and Britain must of course be debited against their internal resources, unless, as may be possible, the indemnity actually obtainable from Germany be taken approximately as an offset. If, as is held likely in some quarters, Britain is induced to write off the debts of her continental Allies, while she continues to bear the burden (largely incurred on their account) of her obligations to the United States, her financial and economic position in the world is proportionately weakened. That weakness will chiefly be manifested in her diminished export of capital and the increasing share in world-development taken by the countries which have been gainers by the war, i.e. the neutrals of Europe, the United States and Japan. The definite passage of the United States from the status of a debtor to that of a creditor nation is a momentous event, not only in its economic but in its political bearings.

Treating population, national resources, developed industry and commerce as the main constituents of world-power, the chief result of the Great War has been the reduction of the power of Germany and France and the enlargement of the power of the United States. Alone among the Western Powers she is free from the crushing burden and anxiety of inflation and indebtedness. She alone is confident of her ability to cope with revolution. The poverty of Mid and Eastern Europe will send her increasing supplies of relatively cheap labour. The crimes and follies of European governments and peoples do not come closely home to her. Her stake as a creditor nation is not so great, and her slight ventures in imperialist exploitation have not yet gone so far, as dangerously to entangle her in the possible debacle of European material and moral civilization. That she will take a growing part in outside affairs as a world-power there can be no doubt. But she is in a mood and a position to choose times and occasions, and to put such limits on her intervention as her interests seem to dictate. The outside world is far more dependent upon her than she upon the outside world. This may not be the case a generation hence, when her foreign trade and overseas investments have woven strong permanent bonds. But her immediate outlook is one of powerful and proud independence.

Apart from this, there are three considerations of outstanding importance in any inspection of the political-economic horizon, viz. the economic recovery of Germany, the economic development of Russia and the business imperialism of Japan. All hinge upon the making of a real peace in Europe, with such provisions for the discharge of foreign debts and for the restoration of the financial and transport facilities of commerce as shall restore social order and set men's minds upon the cultivation of the arts of industry. The powers of healing and recovery are there, provided the returning sanity of governments will give them free play. Given access on fair terms of purchase to her former supplies of coal, iron and potash, and to equal opportunities of foreign trade and emergency credits required to set her industries agoing, there is good reason to believe that the science, industry and discipline which are Germany's most productive assets would put her quickly on the road to recovery, besides enabling her to make large contributions to the restoration of France and Belgium. Though the temporary shortage of capital in Europe would prevent any rapid development of the almost virgin natural resources of Russia, the resumption of commercial relations with other countries would, under the present or any other tolerably settled government, make the exploitation of these resources an exceedingly important factor in economic and political history.

The third problem, which I call the business imperialism of Japan, is in effect the problem of the economic development of China, involving racial issues of the first magnitude, to which I will presently revert. This also is an aspect of the European peace. If no early peace of healing and of restoration is made, no effective steps can be taken to check the process of exclusive and aggressive imperialism which Japan has been pursuing and will continue to pursue in China. It is the greatest remaining opportunity for imperial expansion. The traditional pacifism of China lies nakedly exposed to the militarism and forceful diplomacy of "the Prussia of the East." Europe, weak and concentrated on her own troubles, could not intervene, and apart from any effective League of Nations, the United States would not, provided that the Chinese preoccupation with Japan kept the yellow peoples out of America.

Finally, the development of the South American Republics must not be left out of account. The ABC States already rank as political and economic personages, and for the next few years both Argentina and Brazil will play important parts as owners of essential supplies of which there is a world shortage. It is evident that both the tropical and subtropical countries of South America, which have strengthened their financial conditions during the years of war-prosperity, have definitely risen in the scale of economic and political importance. Sheltered under the wing of the Monroe Doctrine [1] from dangerous entanglements in outside conflicts and nourished by increasing flows of capital from the United States, they are destined to a rapid growth of population and wealth during the coming years.

Indeed, one noteworthy result of the war has been to intensify the movement, observed by economists in the pre-war era, which was steadily turning the balance of commercial gain in favour of countries producing surpluses of foods and raw materials

[1] How much of this Doctrine remains applicable to South American States which have become members of the League of Nations is as yet undetermined.

and against those exporting finished manufactured goods. Attributable to the growing attraction of town life due to the spread of information and cheap transport, the immigration from countries of low national standards of consumption to those of higher standards, such as the United States, the British Dominions and Argentina, and the accompanying rise in standards of living in great and hitherto backward populations, as in India and China, the pace of the movement will now be quicker. The destruction of large quantities of material wealth during the war; the letting down of all stocks of foods and raw materials; the failure of rural labour, diverted into fighting or war-industries, to return to agriculture; the conflicts and disturbances in many countries of Europe and Asia; the enhanced incomes of the working classes in many industrial countries, spent in demand for foods and other consumable goods—all these factors contribute to give scarcity value to raw products, and commercial strength and wealth to countries which have surpluses to sell. Though this temporary gain for the less developed and thinly peopled countries ought to be corrected by stimulating the flow of capital and labour into these more remunerative lands and occupations, this process of adjustment is notoriously slow. The lure of town life and the refusal of rural solitude and dullness, though compensated by more economic independence and higher pay, are one of the most serious problems that confront the world. A later solution may perhaps be found in a stationary population, due to the lower birth-rate of the increasing proportion of town-dwellers and the application of labour-saving machinery and other scientific methods to the cultivation of the soil and other extractive industries. But, for the immediate future, this economic strengthening of backward countries and a proportionate weakening of advanced and highly peopled countries may be a fact of determinant importance.

Western civilized nations and their statecraft have become increasingly conscious of their dependence upon distant lands containing the actual and potential supplies of foods and raw materials. The chief secret driving force in the causation of the Great War was, as we now recognize, the demand for the control of countries which could supply these needs. If any doubt still lingered about the accuracy of this economic interpretation, the scramble of the victorious Allies for mandatory areas will suffice to dissipate it. There seems but one way to avert or modify the costs of the dependence of an advanced country upon backward countries, namely, to secure a political and economic control which shall make the latter its dependents. This is Imperialism.

One clear reflection emerges from this analysis. It is that during the years immediately before us large backward countries, whether absorbed as colonies or protectorates by advanced countries or left in control of their government and economic resources, must play a greater part than hitherto in world economy and world politics.

CHAPTER II

A SHAM LEAGUE OF NATIONS

THESE considerations of the relative strength and wealth of the political divisions of the earth would not have counted heavily if the essential idea inspiring the proposal of a League of Nations had been capable of early realization. For that idea posits a community of interests between nations to be promoted by active conscious co-operation for the common good. This is the positive conception of the League, kept somewhat in the background by a not unnatural stress upon the negative conception of the prevention of war by just settlement of international differences. A real League would have performed two early services of priceless value. It would have realized the urgent and immediate necessity of concerted action between all the advanced nations of the world for a joint administration of the short world supplies of food, materials, fuel, transport and credit, to meet the emergency of the reconstruction period. The chief immediate work of the League would have been this temporary distribution of essential economic supplies according to needs, in complete disregard of war distinctions except so far as reflected in national needs. The performance of this task would have given substance and vitality to the League and secured that moral confidence the failure of which has been adduced as evidence of the futility of the idea. It would have afforded the most striking lesson of interdependence and essential community of interests between nations that history had ever given. The Economic Council of the League would have figured literally as the saviour of whole peoples from starvation, pestilence and anarchy. The second service it could have performed would have been to secure, not merely for the present emergency but for a permanent policy, complete equality of commercial and other economic relations between advanced and backward countries, thus drawing the fangs of competitive imperialism and saving the weaker peoples from oppressive exploitation by removing the *motif* of those pushful foreign policies which lead to war.

The League which might have done this great work was deliberately maimed at birth by its parents. Instead of being founded upon the broad basis of peaceful equality of nations, it was tied as an appendage to a dictated peace, thus absorbing the principle not of equal justice but of force in its very origin. This war-origin impaired its structure and poisoned its functions. It was not a League of Nations, but a League of the Foreign Offices of the Governments of the victorious Allies, with a thin camouflage of picked neutrals. The Council, in which most of the critical judgments and all the administrative power vested, consisted of the great victorious Powers and their nominees. The war-origin was further driven home by the denial at the outset of membership to Germany, Austria and Russia, who were to dwell in outer darkness until they had repented of their sins and established democratic governments satisfactory to their late enemies. The most important and immediate task assigned to the League was the enforcement of an unjust, vindictive and impracticable peace, the intolerable terms of which were breeding wars, famine and misery all over Europe. The wholesome provisions for submitting international differences to equitable methods of adjustment were maimed by the refusal of free and equal access to the League and its Council and Assembly, and by the insistence on the right of the League to interfere in the disputes and difficulties of unrepresented outsiders. Finally, the futility of such a League was enforced by the provision of unanimity for almost all important acts, which enabled France, or any other unbelieving Power, to paralyse the operation of the League.

The same vices of partiality and tyranny, couched in a really nauseating fume of pious professions, stamp the treatment of the mandates under which the subject countries taken from the enemy in the Great War are to be administered. Justice and sound policy impose two obligations in dealing with those "liberated" peoples who are not deemed capable of immediate independence and self-government. The first is that they shall not be handed over to the uncontrolled will of any single civilized Power, but that the League shall exercise a real authority, to determine who shall have the Mandate and on what terms, to exercise by independent reports and agents a constant and effective supervision over the operation of the Mandate, and to change the Mandate or its terms if abuses are shown to exist.

The theory of the Mandate is that it is exercised primarily in the interests of the mandated peoples, who are not to be misgoverned or exploited, and, secondly, in the equal interest of the whole Society of Nations, whose members shall share alike in any benefits accruing from the development of the resources under the good government and education of the Mandatory Power. The latter is to enjoy no special economic priority or privilege, save such as are inseparable from its more intimate contact. The text of the Covenant does imperfect pen-service to the sound theory. The practice of the Allies is a contemptuous violation of it.

If this League were really designed, as its advocates pretend, to be a genuinely international instrument, why should this mandatory principle be confined expressly in its application to "those colonies and territories which, as a consequence of the late war, have ceased to be under the sovereignty of the States which formerly governed them." If the object be to put a check upon selfish imperialism, why should the policy not be of general application in the government of backward peoples?

Again, the mandatory principle, assigning to the League the selection and appointment of the mandatory and the determination of the nature of the mandate, though provided for in Article XXII of the Covenant, has been consistently disregarded by the Allies. By secret bargaining with one another the representatives of the Big Three at Paris, or before, divided up the conquered territories of their enemies among themselves under "mandates," on terms dictated by their respective appetites. The Covenant was expressly doctored to meet the case. German colonies and protectorates claimed by the British Dominions and Japan are simply handed over to be "administered under the Mandatory as integral parts of its territory." Though it is pretended that an account must here be rendered to the League and that the interests of the mandated population are to be safeguarded, no means of making good these formal guarantees exists or can exist.

"Certain communities formerly belonging to the Turkish Empire" are to receive the "administrative advice and assistance of a Mandatory until such time as they are able to stand alone," and it is provided that "the wishes of these communities must be a principal consideration in the selection of the Mandatory." What is actually done? The desirable lots are fought over and shared out among Britain, France and Italy. There is no pretence of any genuine consultation of "the wishes" of these peoples. The process of appointment is a deal, a thing of haggling and of pulls, in which coveted supplies of mineral or vegetable oils, iron, phosphates or rubber, compete with military prestige or frontier defence as determinant factors.[1] It is now openly avowed that the actual disposal of these and the other conquered areas lay, first, with the Ally whose forces conquered them; secondly, with the Supreme Council, and only thirdly, by perfunctory reference, with the League of Nations. The main terms of this deal, indeed, were announced simultaneously with the terms of the German Peace

[1] Cf. Lord Curzon's defence of our position in Mesopotamia, where "obligations of honour and duty, and *even of expediency*, compel us to remain," and where we are obliged to keep 80,000 troops "because of the general situation in the Middle East," i.e. our retention of India (House of Lords, June 26, 1920).

Treaty and long before the League was brought into existence.

The other mandated areas, "especially those in Central Africa," are handed over to the full administration of the Mandatory under conditions alleged to secure the native populations against oppression and demoralization and to "secure equal opportunities for the trade and commerce of other members of the League."

Now, there are three fatal flaws in the mandatory clauses of the Covenant as operated. The first is the branding of this new and delicate organ of a new world-order with the war-origin, and the disposal of the mandated areas as war-spoils by the victors. The second is the futility of the pretence that the vital interests of the mandated populations can be secured by means of annual Reports or appeals to a Council whose judgments must be unanimous and which has no means of enforcing any judgment it may form. The third flaw is the failure to apply the doctrine of the Open Door for the commerce and capital of the world. Only for one of the three groups of mandatory areas is there provision of "equal opportunities for trade and commerce." Even here it is confined to "other members of the League," and the language would be consistent with that preference to the trade of the Mandatory which the policy and usage of all the Mandatories except Britain would enforce. The only other provision looking towards commercial freedom is in Article XXIII, which approves "equitable treatment for the commerce of all nations of the League," but subject to "the provisions of international conventions existing or hereafter to be agreed upon," language which apparently contemplates special "favoured nations" or other preferential arrangements.

The inclusion at the formation of the League of all willing nations, the detachment of the constitution and functions of the League from all war associations, the adoption of open diplomacy and popular representation in the League Government, effective international control over the relations between advanced and backward peoples, the application of the Open Door policy to all backward countries and new areas of economic development—such were the prime essentials for the success of a League of Nations. Could such a League, detached from its poisonous association with the Peace Treaties, have been set up without delay, and put to the immediate task of devising an emergency international finance, transport and commerce for the period of reconstruction, its moral capital would soon have been raised to a figure which would have enabled it to undertake its other permanent duties, of conserving peace, reducing armaments and promoting active co-operation for the health, wealth, knowledge and moral progress of nations, with a measure of success that would have astonished humanity.

This perversion of this great ideal of a League of Nations into a present instrument for autocratic and imperialistic government will rank in history as a treason to humanity as deplorable as the Peace Treaty with which it was so injuriously bound.

The first inevitable result has been to pour discredit upon the League and the idea it professes but fails to embody. Great statesmen have vied in their contempt for it. There is an obstinate clinging to armed Alliances, of which the new attempted compact between France, Britain and America, only thwarted by the refusal of America, was a conspicuous instance.

Why has the League failed to materialize? Not only the moral idealism but the obvious material interests of every country appeared to be enlisted in its behalf. Its success alone could save the world from slipping back into the old mire. What blocked success? The first answer is quite plain. The fears and greeds of inflamed nationalism. France, Italy, Japan, Greece, Poland, Roumania, Czecho-Slovakia and Jugo-Slavia are all bent on schemes of territorial expansion which make any scheme of pacific internationalism impracticable, while Britain's new imperialism, under the guise of mandates, renders her leadership in any League of Nations suspect.

CHAPTER III

THE ACHIEVEMENT OF DEMOCRACY

WHY has the League started wrong? Because it is a League not of Peoples but of Governments. Yet nearly all the member States enjoy the forms of popular self-government. Why, then, is it not a League of Peoples operated through their chosen representatives? The answer, already foreshadowed in our analysis of social unrest, is that nowhere is the People in effective control of its Government.

In other words, the failure of Internationalism runs back to the failure of Democracy. Has the war done anything for Democracy? It has destroyed several absolutist monarchies. The "king business" is reduced to small dimensions—to Britain, Italy and Spain alone among the larger States. Everywhere monarchy is dead or dying. The world has now become overwhelmingly republican in constitution China, Russia, Germany, Austria, Hungary, Jugo-Slavia, Czecho-Slovakia have taken on the forms of a democratic republic. Monarchy can hardly be said to be a real factor in the government of our Overseas Dominions, which are in substance and in spirit republican. Monarchy stands there as a purely sentimental relic.

More important than the collapse of monarchism

is the collapse of the policy and organization of Liberalism. In Britain, in America and, though less decisively, in the industrially developed countries of the Continent, a large bourgeoisie of petty employers and traders, with the main body of the professional classes, formed a solid phalanx of support for a moderate progressive policy. The concentration of industry and finance upon the one hand, the growth of workers' organizations upon the other, were weakening this main support of Liberalism during the last generation. But its downfall has been hastened by the experiences of the war. The cautious and unprincipled opportunism upon which it had lived so long is discredited as a policy hopelessly incompetent to cope with the live issues of our time, and its economic prosperity is damaged by a redistribution of income in which it cannot hope to hold its own against the upper and the nether pressures to which it is everywhere subjected. Profiteering, high wages and taxation threaten its existence.

This decline of the economic and political power of the middle classes might appear to be the natural precursor of a proletarian domination. Everywhere the broadening of the franchise has moved towards adult suffrage. In some of the advanced countries women have a vote on equal terms with men, and in others victory for their cause is within sight. The peoples everywhere thus appear to hold in their hands the instruments of good self-government.[1]

[1] But will our proletariat better than the middle classes fulfil the conditions of successful government which Matthew Arnold, through the mouth of his German critic, "Armenius," desiderated?—"The era of aristocracies is over: nations must now stand or fall by the intelligence of the middle classes and their people. The people with you is still an embryo; no one can yet say what

Their freely elected representatives make the laws and can, if they choose, appoint and control those who administer the laws, they can determine the conduct both of domestic and of foreign policy and hold in their hands the purse-strings of the nations. Such is the theory. But friends and enemies of Democracy alike know that in practice it is a failure. Neither through the electoral machinery nor by the more informal exercise of public opinion has the people any adequate control over its Government. This disillusionment regarding the democratic experiment is widespread and deep. Many men of liberal proclivities are so much disconcerted by its failure that they are disposed to accept Hegel's judgment, "The public is that part of the State which does not know what it wants." Others would take the more lenient view that the popular will is outwitted and set aside by the play of particular interests. Others, again, are so deeply impressed by the lightness and unwisdom of the popular will, as it does emerge and seek to express itself in policy, that their mind drifts towards some form of that doctrine of benevolent aristocracy which has haunted so many superior minds.

"In a democracy the real rulers are the dexterous manipulators of votes, with their placemen, the mechanics who so skilfully operate the hidden springs which move the puppets in the arena of democratic elections." Thus wrote the Russian arch-reactionary Pobyedonostsev. But his judgment is endorsed and illustrated with a wealth of

it will come to. You lean, therefore, with your whole weight upon the intelligence of your middle class. And intelligence, in the true sense of the word, your middle class has absolutely none" (*Friendship's Garland*).

instances in the remarkable exposures of American and British electoral institutions by Ostrogorski and Graham Wallas, and would be received with a pretty general acceptance by serious students of politics in these and other democratic countries, including the British Dominions, in which democratic forms have been applied under conditions *prima facie* more favourable to success than those prevailing in the older countries.

There are those who, imputing the failure to the complexity of democratic machinery, would have recourse to direct government, through the Referendum and Initiative and the Recall, while others again would seek the cure by concentrating authority and responsibility upon a single elected person.[1] But though certain abuses of electoral power, corrupt deals with business interests, appointment of incompetent officials, dishonest finance and direct violations of electoral pledges may be curbed by such methods, none of them goes to the root of the failure. Lack of knowledge and feebleness of organization are the underlying causes of the unreality and incompetence of a popular will. Behind both, it will be urged, lies lack of interest. If the ordinary man and woman took as much interest in politics as they take in sport and recreation, in business and in domestic life, if politics were as real to them as are these things, we should have an effective democracy. Now, it used to be true that politics were unreal in the sense of being unimportant, that is to say, not dealing with vital issues. This is

[1] These two opposite cures for the corruption and incompetence of ordinary electoral institutions are in active competition, or sometimes in conjunction, in various States and Municipal Governments of America.

no longer true. Everybody to-day knows that the great happenings in which governments and politicians are engaged come home directly, in cost and risk of person and of property, to everyone. But there still remains the feeling that the public concern is not in any true sense my concern, the persons who do these things are in no sense under my control. Public opinion, so far as it exists, may be against the Government, may fear and even hate its goings on. But it is impotent. Why? Partly, no doubt, for lack of confidence in the sufficiency and reliability of its knowledge of facts. Public opinion thus suffers from want of information. But its impotence is chiefly due to the fact that it is not "public" in any sense that implies close unity and effective co-operation. Public opinion is little more than the aggregate of private opinions formed separately and functioning separately.

So far as lack of information goes, that would seem to be curable by better education, more curiosity about affairs and a more informed criticism of the news and opinions laid before the public. But here we enter perhaps the most vicious of all the circles that imprison us. Better education might go far, but the enemies of Democracy can see to it that education is bad. And this they do. Instinctively they have long recognized that sound news and serious thinking are dangerous, and the schools, the Press and even the churches which they control are used as safeguards. By selection and rejection of teachers, preachers, editors and writers, by manipulation of news, opinions and formulas, they succeed in making the public want what they hold it desirable the public should want. These processes are now generalized into an art of propaganda, and there is for the first time a quite open recognition by the ruling and possessing classes everywhere that every organ of public opinion can and should be utilized by them in self-defence against the dangerous movements which are trying to make Democracy a real government of the people. The conservation of the interests figures as patriotism, loyalty and morality. These emotional dopes they combine with a profitable support for the recreations and amusements which distract and dissipate the general mind. To keep this mind at the low level of instruction and attention which makes it most suggestible and plastic, and then to ply it with the right suggestions—this is the now accepted policy of class defence. Since every organ of this propagandism is a department of the capitalist State, or of big business, or of capitalist philanthropy, direct resistance is well-nigh impossible. This diagnosis of propaganda will only seem exaggerated to those who are ignorant of the intricacy of the pressures which mould the instruction of our schools and universities, our newspapers, our churches, theatres, music-halls and cinemas. The schoolroom, the Press and the cinema are the modern power-houses of a low and frivolous mentality. Out of the suggestions and stimuli thus imposed is generated that mob-mind whose ignorant, violent and capricious working is then adduced as proof of the inherent inability of the people to undertake the real duties of government.

We began this analysis by asking why a real League of Nations failed to come into being when the needs of humanity so plainly called for it. We now see that Internationalism in any true sense stands upon the foundation of a national Democracy, and that this Democracy in its turn rests upon a popular will which cannot function under existing conditions of capitalist control in the world of politics and business.

This point has been often reached. It is now accepted ground that political democracy is impossible without industrial democracy. But what is industrial democracy? It is not State Socialism under existing forms of Parliamentary government in which the ownership and operation of essential industries shall be vested in officials at Westminster. Such centralized bureaucracy is no longer acceptable in any quarter. Such Nationalization is as unpopular with labour as with capital. State management is thoroughly discredited. Post-war movements converge upon proposals of industrial reconstruction which seek to sever ownership from operation. The capital structure of an industry may be taken over by the State, or may remain in private ownership with or without some State guarantee of dividends, or may even pass into possession of the employees. But the management of the industry is to be in the hands of a body representing those whose activities contribute to the value of the product. I choose these words because just at this point grave misunderstandings are likely to arise. For, ignoring the narrower and more ignorant interpretation of industrial self-government which would place the management entirely in the hands of the manual wage-workers on the ground that they are the only real producers, we meet the syndicalism which would vest the power entirely in the brain and hand workers, the body of directly active operators of the industry. Capital is here treated as purely static, a condition, not an efficient cause in processes of production. Labour alone is dynamic.

But the capital structure of an industry is not static: fresh supplies are needed for its enlargement and improvement, and those who provide these supplies must have some inducement to provide them and some guarantee that they will not be wasted. In other words, capital will claim representation in the Board of Management. The naïve proposal to sever ownership from management evidently cannot work, whether private investment or public revenue be the source from which new capital be drawn. The claim that the State shall be the owner of the mines, the railways and other plant, and shall supply more additional capital as it is wanted, but shall hand over the complete control of the operation to the staff and workers, is not seriously arguable. Whether the State or private investors are to be the owners of the industrial plant and other capital, it is evident that industrial self-government demands their participation in the management. Nor does that exhaust the claimants. Any true account of the operation of an industry from the standpoint of the value of its product cannot ignore the market, the consumer. The constant play of the force of demand issuing from the consumer is an important factor in determining the processes of production and needs recognition in the government of every industry.

Labour of brain and hand, capital and the market, are all dynamic factors in an industry, and those who own and apply them in production must all have a voice in management. Only thus can an industry become genuinely self-governing. The autocratic government of industry by the owners of the capital, who hitherto have claimed to buy their labour-power and their ability, as they bought their raw materials, and to use them as mere instruments for private profiteering, cannot be replaced by the wider autocracy of labour claiming to buy the capital, ability and raw materials they need, in order to use these as mere instruments for private gains to labour. Nor can the issue be compromised by admitting the specialized ability within the industry to a share of the control and gains. Self-government demands that all the live factors be represented. Capital, however provided, whether by private saving and investment or by public appropriation, remains a live factor, which will not do its work without recognition of its vitality. If the State, i.e. the whole body of citizen-taxpayers, is to provide it, then the State must have an official voice in every board of management. And so with the consumer. If the legitimate checks and controls of the market are to be operative, it will not suffice that the consumers' interests be represented through the capital-owning State. The special needs and character of markets will differ in various industries, and methods of direct representation must be found for them, if industrial democracy is to be soundly established. We in Britain are beginning to march along this road of industrial democracy. For here the defensive forces of the propertied and ruling interests are already divided. Breaches have already been made in these defences by concessions to the demand of the workers for a definite participation in the management of important public or other highly organized industries. So long as these concessions halt at the level of a Whitley Council, their meaning can be concealed, for they appear nothing more than slight extensions of the voluntary Boards for Conciliation or Arbitration with which big industry has long been familiar. But the proposals of the Sankey Report on the Coal Mines and the governmental Bill for the management of Railways have introduced into two great industries the definitely new principle of representative government, with such controls as profess to eliminate the autocracy and the profiteering which are the essence of capitalism.

Indeed, the whole post-war emergency policy of regulating wages, prices and profits, if it be maintained, must undermine capitalism in every trade where it is applied. This attack on capitalism, as we have seen, is the result of a number of converging movements accelerated by the war. The concentration of capital and the substitution of combination for competition have gone so far in many of the great industries as to present the menace of profiteering monopolies in the essentials of national life. The competitive system is worked out, and the alternatives of public and private monopoly emerge. The combinations of labour in these same industries, partly by industrial, partly by political action, have forced up the standard wages, hours and other conditions of employment to levels which in some whole industries, such as railways, and in parts of others, such as mining, render their profitable working, even upon the lowest level of remuneration of capital, no longer feasible. Modern governments are more and more committed to support standards of life for the workers which involve definite encroachments upon the older rights of capital. On the other hand, the consuming public, normally impotent, has under the stress of high prices and short supplies become so urgent in its demand for regulated prices, that capital can no longer count on passing on to the consumer with an extra profit the new costs of production.

But will capitalism, thus undermined, give place to the genuinely representative government here indicated, or will an era of proletarian domination intervene? The Soviet experiment in Russia has undoubtedly met responses in the temper of certain revolutionary forces in Western countries. The Marxian determinism of the class war between the sharply defined forces of labour and capital, in which the power of bourgeois capitalism shall be displaced by the power of the proletariat, has its votaries in every country. Most of them argue that this transformation will be brought about by the blind violence of the workers, inspired and directed by the will of a small class-conscious minority, and expressing itself through strikes, sabotage and, if necessary, armed conflict. Their philosophy of history teaches them that such force is the only effective weapon for the overthrow of an existing rule, and the proletariat intends to use it. After it has conquered capitalism and the capitalist State, it will establish a pacific "ergatocracy" upon a just basis of representation, in which functional shall replace regional representation.

Can we be certain that the main body of organized labour in the West may not be so strongly attracted by this teaching and practice as to plunge their countries into a Soviet revolution? The time may seem favourable. For six years the world has tacitly abrogated all authority of reason and justice and accepted force as the arbiter of human affairs. The same force which ruled in war still rules in peace. The world has been reorganized on a basis of force. Every Western country is filled with returned warriors whose character has been "made over" by the force-discipline, while civil society has been steeped in the spectatorial lust of violence. The disposition to revert to force in the settlement of every sort of dispute has been manifested everywhere. How can labour get its right by any other method than a class war conducted under the same rule of force?

It is evident that here, in France, and especially in America, there is a widespread fear of the class war, and a humorously foolish attempt to stop it by anticipatory measures of force. For thus, according to the Marxist gospel, the declining force of capitalism encounters the rising force of proletarianism.

The accepted theory of civilization was that force as a determinant of conduct was continually in process of elimination. War has endowed it with a new prestige and made every movement correspondingly explosive. It is not armed violence that is alone in question. It is economic force. It is arbitrary will in government, unreasoning authority in education and religion and morals, the cult of violence in art and literature under the guise of nature and of spontaneity. The adaptation of science to purposes of violence has wrought upon the nerves of mankind with terrible suggestiveness. No wonder it has gained vogue in the world of labour.

But if we turn in sober earnest to assess the danger of the red revolution which is announced, it dwindles to small dimensions. What is this force with which a class-conscious minority is to overthrow capitalism and to destroy the capitalist State? Does it exist in France, here or in America? The workers, indeed, are everywhere the great majority. Their united action could everywhere prevail. But the workers are not all proletariat. In France and America, even in Britain, a large population are farmers or peasants with some stake in the land, thrifty and conservative. In town and country independent artisans and other small producers and traders abound. A revolutionary strike of town-workers could and would be starved out by the refusal of the country-folk to supply food. This happens even in Russia, where the peasants have been bought into the revolution by distribution of the land. But neither is there full solidarity in the ranks of the town wage-workers. The black-coated proletariat of the shops, warehouses and offices has a widely different mentality from the industrial proletariat, and is far more feebly organized. Not more than one-third of the wage-earning classes even in Britain is unionized, and the proportion is far smaller in America and France. Craft unionism still prevails in many industries, dividing skilled from unskilled workers, and retaining specialist interests which impair the unity of industrial action. In Britain the possibility of successful revolutionary force lies in the solidarity of a few powerful labour combinations in essential industries, notoriously in the group known as the Triple Alliance, with the engineering trades as an auxiliary. These unions, it is contended, hold the keys of economic life in every nation, and could therefore dictate terms to nations and governments. But how? By stopping essential supplies of goods and services. By this stoppage, however, they suffer equally with the rest of the community, and the resentment of the whole community is directed against them. For experience shows that direct action, taken by the whole or any part of this group, does not in fact arouse the sympathy but the antagonism of the generality of workers, even in the other organized trades. It is indeed possible, perhaps probable, that a general sympathy of working-class opinion might support a regular strike of the Triple Alliance in redress of a definite industrial grievance. But a revolutionary strike for the overthrow of the capitalist system and the mastery of the State could count upon no body of outside support. Nay, as recent tentative experiments have shown, it could not command the general support of the rank and file of the Triple Alliance, even were the wider revolutionary design covered by the narrower purpose of frustrating a hated action of the Government. Neither in numbers nor in solidarity can the requisite proletarian force be found in Britain. And in America and France the case for force is weaker.

Again, the force at the disposal of capitalism and the capitalist State is depreciated by a shallow bluff. The soldiery, the police, the blacklegs, upon whom capitalism relies in the last resort to crush the proletarian revolution, are themselves, it is contended, proletarian and would desert their paymasters. And there are circumstances where this argument holds good. A corrupt, incompetent and visibly oppressive bureaucracy, like that of the late Tsardom, lost the allegiance of its mercenaries. But the prestige of the Western pseudo-democratic States is still unimpaired in the minds of the vast majority of their officials and employees, and discipline is strongly maintained. While, therefore, it is possible to conceive a situation in which soldiery or police would refuse to protect blacklegs in working railways or in carrying out martial law, that situation would take the character of some concrete local quarrel where public passion was aroused against some special act of governmental tyranny. But, even so, such sporadic sympathy would go but a very little way towards the wide project of a proletarian revolution.

There is no evidence of the existence of a revolutionary disposition in the mass of the organized workers of this country or America. The pretence that it does exist is due to the interaction of a double propaganda of a dramatic inflammatory order, the missionary energy of little revolutionary groups on the one hand, the inoculatory scares of the capitalist Press upon the other. These two *motifs* play into one another's hands so as to give an exaggerated importance to the revolutionary movement and to credit it with a force which it does not possess. The modern economy of force under scientific control has admittedly diminished the value of numbers for revolutionary action. The capitalist order retains in its service the great majority of men skilled in the scientific use of force: they are attached to it by bonds of sympathy and interest, and most of those who might be won over to a proletarian movement would belong to the pacifist wing of that movement.

It is to the interest of capitalism and the capitalist State to keep the class war upon the plane of physical and economic force. This has two advantages for them. It enables them to rally all the conservative elements in the community in support of a militarism which enables them to preserve order at home and to execute a pushful and a profitable foreign policy. Still more important, it disables the proletariat from using the emotional and intellectual forces wherein their true strength lies.

Only when the illusion of the efficiency of physical force as the instrument of progress is dispelled can a real Democracy become possible. For only then can full and conscious use be made of those powers of social idealism which we found embedded in the instincts of mankind, the biological urge towards wider human co-operation and solidarity.

CHAPTER IV

SELF-DETERMINATION AND FEDERALISM

THE war has contributed two conspicuous services to the formulation of the art of social progress. One is the costly exhibition of the futility of force. The other is the dramatic assertion of the doctrine of self-determination. Both in origin and in meaning self-determination is the antithesis of force. It has been lifted into politics from the realm of personal ethics. There it implies the power of a person to guide his conduct in each particular case by consideration of the permanent good of the whole self instead of by the satisfaction of some single passing desire. Self is raised from the narrow range of a short-sighted selfishness to the dimensions of a full human personality while determination implies the sovereignty of an informed and reasonable will. These same implications follow the application of the term as a principle of national or group conduct. A self-determining community is one that acts and lives by the conscious exercise of a collective will, directed to the general permanent good and secure from external interference in the performance of this self-regarding duty. The rule of force in its ultimate analysis means the direction of conduct by single unregulated impulses and desires. Self-determination means the co-ordination and co-operation of impulses and desires in conformity with a conscious plan.

The first condition of such co-operation is, of course, a substantial unity of selfhood. Even in the sphere of individual psychology the problem of dissociated personality, with double and opposed determination, sometimes arises. As Paul so well recognized, there may be not only rebellious desires but opposed systems of desire within the confines of a single mind. But, in nations or other social groupings, the delimitation of the self is much more difficult. Almost every historical nation has its Ulster, a larger or smaller fragment, more or less compact, and stronger or weaker in its demand to be treated as a separate self in the determination of its government. And scrupulous analysis will discover fresh fissures within each separate self, carrying the process towards anarchy. But such difficulties of delimitation do not invalidate the principle or policy. Areas of effective autonomy are ascertainable.

There is, however, a more important aspect of the problem, involving a limitation of the application of the principle itself. Selves are never completely separate.

Man is a social animal in such a sense and degree that all his thoughts, feelings and actions are affected by and in their turn affect those of the fellow-members of his group. Similarly with groups or national selves. They cannot live alone. Here the dangers of an absolutist view of self-determination are manifest. The economic interdependence of nations is the most obvious limitation of national self-determination. Never has it been more startlingly illustrated than in the fatal effects of the sudden severance of economic relations between the new nations into which Austro-Hungary has been resolved. But nations do not live by bread alone. The intellectual and moral interdependence of nations is a prime factor in civilization. That interdependence must be recognized in the field of politics by some formal bonds of association which shall definitely qualify the principle of self-determination.

The principle of federalism must qualify the principle of self-determination. This is the harmony of unity and diversity as it shows itself in every field of conduct. Autonomy so far as aims and ends are separate, union so far as they are identical. Federation connotes the political harmony of the opposing principles. Upon every scale of social co-operation, from the family to humanity, the problem is continually before us. All our institutions are in process of recasting by fresh attempts to apply the federal principle.

In politics its action is of a twofold and contrary character. The wrongs and wastes of over-centralization are remedied by devolution, while a growing community of interests between the parts of a political system strengthens the federal bond. Both of these movements are active at the present time in a reconstitution of the British Empire. The new problem of the League of Nations involves, therefore, the introduction of no new political principle, but only an extension of that moving force of mutuality of interests which has everywhere and always been operative upon smaller areas.

The vital issues of economics are not essentially different. Individualism versus Socialism, Combination versus Competition, present the problem in its most abstract form. But each practical problem, the co-operation of the several factors of production within the workshop, the department, the plant, the business, the trade, the relation of the several workshops, departments, plants in a single business, and of the businesses within a trade, and finally the relations of interdependency between different trades —the whole matter of the orderly structure and functioning of business embodies the same problem of a harmony which is physical in relation to its material parts, moral in its arrangement of motives and incentives.

But the challenge to reconstruction or revolution by a conscious application of the principles of self-determination and federation is by no means confined to the field of politics and economics. Every social institution needs recasting in the light of the new demands which war reveals or produces. Specialism and generalism in the acquisition and communication of knowledge is a burning question for education: division of labour, it is commonly agreed, has gone dangerously far and needs correction by the enforcement of the unity of knowledge. Religion is similarly confronted with the wasteful economy of sectarianism and the demand for a new catholicism. Even within the family the close patriarchy is yielding to the demand for something like a federal republic.

The term "federation" will, of course, cover many diverse forms and degrees of union and divergency, of liberty and restraint. But the principle should gain conscious acceptance everywhere as our guide. For better than any other it expresses the moving compromise between the opposite demands of the narrower and the wider urges of man. And amid all the wild excesses and the tumult of our present world this moving compromise mus be regarded as the actual process of Nature in the moulding of human conduct and institutions.

There is, however, an important difference between what we have recognized as the two guiding principles of self-determination and of federation. The former presents itself as a rule of active and energetic process, the latter as a form of structure. The true picture of social evolution shows a series of expanding selves finding their determination in some federal form. The hard-shell egoism of the individual man finds itself both restrained and expressed in the federation of the family. The family, its habitat and income, form a unit of self-interest and of rights within the federal self-government of a city and a State, though, as we ascend to the wider circles of political structure, the federal arrangements ramify into what we may almost term a federal tissue, so intricate becomes the texture of the compromises between narrower and wider selves or areas of conduct.

When we reflect that this same web of association applies to all other human relations besides those termed political, that all our religious, intellectual, philanthropic, business, recreational and "social" world is held together by the same intricate tissue of qualified co-operation among persons or narrower groups for specified purposes, we begin to realize the sanity of the commonplace that "life consists of compromise."

Every one of our pressing problems of to-day consists in the quick need of finding some new functional and structural compromise to replace one whose balance has been upset. The term "compromise" is not, of course, quite adequate, for it has acquired a meaning hostile to "principle." And yet no better term exists to connote the provisional harmony which alone is possible in an ever-changing world.

But in seeking to realize the urge of life, which makes these changes, we shall rightly turn to the fuller meaning of self-determination, the energetic process by which the narrower and wider selves function in the weaving of this federal tissue. And there we come back to that play of the racial or social instincts, impulses and desires, whose longer sweep of biological purpose has been constantly engaged in curbing and controlling the sharp drive of the impulses and desires which make for purely individual and immediate satisfactions. In primitive society we saw these socializing, civilizing impulses checking the individual in his selfish pursuit of his own immediate ends, by imposing on him usages and rudimentary laws needed for the protection and furtherance of the tribe, or other group, of which he was a member. The parental and gregarious instincts we recognized as conveying a social urge strictly biological in its first purpose and not necessarily represented in clear consciousness. The early weaving of social tissue was perhaps no more purposive than the work of beavers in dam-making or of bees in the economy of the hive. The creative play of this social evolution lay perhaps wholly below the level of both individual and general will, and certainly implied no conscious striving for any preconceived goal. This social power was felt by the individual man, partly in the form of restraints upon certain selfish impulses, partly in the form of satisfaction of the primitive social instincts. But, whatever names we give to the race-preserving instincts and emotions, we must regard them as the efficient causes of the whole fabric of society. As men began to be aware and to reflect upon these instinctive urges, law and politics, religion and ethics began to emerge, as arts consciously using these urges and often diverting them into narrower interested channels. In one sense the whole modern struggle for reform may be represented truly as a return to Nature, in that it strives to rescue the resources "intended" for the racial preservation and progress from the selfish exploitation of individuals, groups, classes or nations. The clear recognition of the nature of these selfish perversions of the social instincts and emotions is a distinctively modern process. It has brought into clear relief the inner meaning of Capitalism, Imperialism, Militarism, Protectionism and their related principles and policies, and has exposed their common character. But, by doing so, it has necessarily overstressed the critical and combative work of reform, to the detriment of the constructive and creative. The best way to break the forces of reactionary exploitation is to set the newly liberated social consciousness to the weaving of sound social tissue.

CHAPTER V

THE MUTABILITY OF HUMAN NATURE

If reformers can indicate with clear consciousness the moulds of the new society and the channels by which the creative forces may pour into them, they will evade much of the painful and demoralizing effort of the conflict in which the forces of creative evolution have been wasted in the past.

This is where reason comes in as the great ally of social feeling. If the processes of self-determination and of federation can be raised to the level of a conscious art, using experience as the groundwork of experiment, and social impulse as the warrant for faith in ideals, pacific revolutions may be attainable. For only thus can " the great bluff " about the immutability of Human Nature be " called." Upon the great bluff the intellectual defence of conservatism and reactionism entirely rests. " Human Nature being what it is " industry can only work by offering profitable prizes to energetic business men and giving them an arbitrary power in management. " Human Nature being what it is " working men will only produce efficiently under the whip of economic necessity administered by private capitalism. " Human Nature being what it is " war remains an eternal factor, and all pretences to abolish it are dangerous delusions. This Bluff even calls to its aid the admissions of modern psychology that the original outfit of instincts and emotions with which primitive man was equipped cannot have been greatly modified during the brief process of civilization and must still constitute the urge of human life.

This issue of the mobility of Human Nature is, however, misrepresented. Progress, even those rapid changes called revolutions, does not depend upon alterations in the psycho-physical make up of man. Such alterations, of course, do take place under the pressure of the forces of environmental and sexual selection. The make-up of the man and woman best fitted to survive and reproduce their kind in modern societies differs perhaps considerably from that best fitted for these purposes in primitive society. But that process of change, it may fairly be contended, must be general and slow, and cannot suffice to give a rationale for those sudden mutations of social structure we are investigating. It is not, however, necessary to assert that the physical, intellectual or moral make-up of a modern infant in a civilized country differs at birth to any appreciable extent from that of the cave-child. It suffices to point out that from the moment of birth through the entire process of nurture, education and experience, the effective or operative nature of the child is undergoing great and numerous changes by the repression and disuse of certain elements of the inherited outfit, the nourishment and use of others, and by the union of certain elements into strong dispositions. It is to this power of selection, rejection and combination of primal instincts that we must look to justify our faith in the work of social transformation that lies before us. In the realm of economics we have to show that private profiteering and the present capitalist structure are wasteful, because they provide excessive but unreliable incentives to the performance of certain useful functions, encouraging some useless or injurious functions while denying adequate incentives to other productive functions. Or, turning to the creative side, we have to show how better business structures can be formed, which, stressing differently the same elements of human nature, will get a stronger and more reliable co-operation of productive forces. Similarly in the realm of politics, constitutional reforms expressing new balances or harmonies of power find their justification in rearrangements of the motive-forces available for political conduct. The case for the alleged necessity of war is crucial. War has virtually disappeared within the smaller social areas of the city, province, nation, by the extension of the federal economy. This federalizing process, with its pacific results, has made an obstinate halt at the stage of nationalism, and all the forces of sociality have been pressed into the service of an exclusive and combative patriotism. But is this social instinct for war, as it appears, an immutable factor in human nature? Are the political forces of association incapable of passing the barriers of State?

It has been ingeniously urged that the final stage of federation of the world is impracticable, because no final outlet would then be given for that fighting instinct which it has only been possible to repress within the narrower areas by concentrating it upon less frequent but bloodier conflicts in the wider areas. This raises in its most dramatic form the question of the pace at which "reason" can alter human nature as an operative concern. If reason cannot abolish war upon its larger scale, civilization seems doomed to early extinction. If this conviction be generally accepted, will that acceptance give us any sufficient power to make a League of Nations or some other arrangement that can stop war? Must the fighting instinct, remaining in its primitive form intact, wreck any arrangement made for its control?

But several questions are here begged. Cannot instincts and the organs necessary for their expression be atrophied by disuse? Will not the absence of any easy opportunity for the exercise of an instinct weaken it? Are boys in a well-ordered modern school, furnished with all sorts of other interests, as much disposed to fisticuffs as in an old-fashioned school? If a League of Nations could be fairly set on foot, with sufficient faith in its successful working to effect a general reduction of armaments, would not the *flair* and prestige of war burn more dimly in the patriotism of each nation?

Finally, assuming that it is not possible thus to enfeeble or repress the combative instinct, may not its activity be diverted into some less destructive or even into some humanly serviceable channel? Many forms of sport or play admittedly are outlets for this instinct, partly for the human elements of conflict they contain, partly by furnishing, in the shape of refractory material or conditions to be overcome, the substitute for a human enemy. But in more spiritual fields of adventure, also, in pitting one's force of physical endurance, intellect or will, in a war against disease and poverty, or in wresting from Nature her hard-held secrets, it may be possible to find what Professor William James called " moral equivalents for war."

The same reasoning applies to industrial incentives. There is no warrant for the assumption that capitalism must be maintained because an immutable law of Human Nature has ordained that the desire for accumulation of property is the only motive adequate to evoke the efforts necessary for the economic maintenance of life. It is neither necessary nor wise for those who question the validity of this assumption to maintain that, by some sudden transformation of the economic system the incentive of social service can be directly substituted for personal gain. It is far more important to undermine the part which property plays in what we may call the economy of egoism. What the self-seeking person is after is self-glory, the realization to himself of his self-importance. Property is an important instrument in this realization for two reasons, first, because it is the conventional badge of worldly success, secondly, because it is a means of exercising power over other people. Since this first value largely depends upon the second, we may conclude that the satisfaction of the acquisitive instinct mainly consists in realizing one's own will as forcibly prevailing over the wills of other persons. Property has, of course, other attractions in the form of sensual and moral satisfactions, but it is this self-glory that is the chief incentive to its acquisition. Now, if this sense of self-importance can be satisfied in other ways, through alterations of the economic system, it may be possible to dispense with profiteering as an incentive. If it can be shown that, with the disappearance of effective competition and the substitution of combination, profiteering becomes continually more wasteful and more dangerous, that the really productive functions of the inventor, organizer, manager, skilled workman can be sustained and stimulated, partly by better regulated gains, partly by interest and pride in work, partly by improved opportunity of rising to positions of importance, may it not be possible to substitute better modes of egoistic self-realization for worse? How much economic value can be attached to the sense of social service, or how rapidly that motive may be strengthened, are questions which only admit of an answer when we see what sort of new society is emerging. At present all we can safely say is that a conscious widespread resentment against working for private profit is visibly impairing the efficiency of labour, and that this must count as an argument for change. On the other hand, it is generally agreed that a mere transfer of management from private company to State bureaucracy would not lead to more efficient labour, probably to less. If social service is to be made an effective economic incentive, it can only be done by appealing to some closer and more actual social feeling than that furnished by a distant abstract entity such as State or Government.

But whether economic reconstruction depends more upon changes in the forms of egoistic appeal or upon strengthening the social as against the egoistic motives is not the really vital issue. For these illustrations drawn from war and industry are designed to present a direct challenge to the central argument of reactionism, the alleged immutability of Human Nature.

Now Human Nature, we see, is mutable, not merely in the sense that natural selection and rejection alter the hereditary make-up by shifting the conditions of the biological competition so as to raise or depress the survival-value of different ingredients in the earlier make-up. Such changes in the substance of the human stock will be for the most part slow and gradual. The great mutations or transformations in effective Human Nature will be attained by changes in education and environment, which, taking human inheritance as it is, alters its operative character by feeding and stimulating certain instincts and emotions, starving and repressing others. Nor is it a matter only of acting upon separate instincts and emotions. New combinations or fusions may be made, altering what is called the disposition or the character. In religious experience we are familiar with the phenomenon of conversion, which may involve an entirely new precipitation of spiritual elements, carrying radical alterations of conduct. Where the stimulus which wrought this conversion is abnormal and momentary in its application, the conversion may not last—the subject may easily fall back into his old ways. But were such conversion a quick adjustment to a new permanent environment, steadily applying new stimuli to the appropriate instincts in Nature's outfit, what is known in biology as a genuine mutation may occur.

So far I have placed this issue in a distinctively biological setting, treating the motives of politics, industry and other branches of human conduct as rooted in physical instincts. But this is not the whole story of the dynamics of human conduct. These alterations of education and environment, to which we may look for quick changes in effective Human Nature, are themselves the products of reason. The disparagement of reason and its scientific work, upon the ground that the power-house of conduct is the emotional equipment of instincts and desires, and that reason is a mere tool of our desires, finding us arguments for doing what we want, is based upon a misunderstanding. "Reason" or the exploring curiosity of man, is a part of his original outfit, endowed with the biological utility of enabling him to effect vital gains and avoid fatal injuries by a better knowledge of his environment. This better knowledge enables him not only to obey Nature but to command her, in the sense of effecting changes beneficial to his life. This exploring process that leads to discovery and invention in the external environment can, however, be turned on to the field of Human Nature itself. The arts of political and economic invention are now perceived to be of paramount importance, and in these arts the exploring intellect must direct itself more and more to institutional reforms which shall react on Human Nature by directing its instincts and emotions along new channels of individual and social behaviour. This is the most delicate and critical work of the inventive or creative power of man. The processes of this invention or creation are primarily intellectual, but the stuff which the intellect uses for this work is the dynamic and directive energy of instinct and desire.

The war has led men to a swift recognition of the obsoleteness or inefficiency of many of our established social institutions. Its shocks have rendered some of them unworkable, or have laid them in ruins across the path of progress. Not one of them but stands in urgent need of fundamental change. Church, State, Property, Industry, Education, the

Family, not one can be rebuilt upon the old foundations. The sole alternative to a wild upheaval, in which the separate passions and group interests shall scramble for blind satisfaction, is an appeal to reason as the preserver of social sanity and the vindicator of the deeper and enduring purposes of mankind. For reason is not a cold-blooded logic. It is humanity moved by its deepest and broadest current of creative energy, working for the largest human ends. The disinterested quality of its work does not exclude emotion. It only excludes the separatist interests from usurping the interest of the whole.

For the driving force of reason as the arbiter and guide of conduct is derived from the race-preserving and race-raising instincts which achieve the social as distinguished from the individual ends of man, and, ever enlarging in the scope and complexity of their operation, involve as their goal the ever-widening ideal of the welfare of humanity.

CHAPTER VI

PROBLEMS OF THE NEW WORLD

THIS conception of the general well-being we recognize to be the substance and the vindication of idealism. To make reason prevail is thus synonymous with social idealism. Against this wider passion of the whole the narrower passions of individuals and groups are continually at war. Every such conflict is a moral struggle, in which the narrower and more concentrated forces, mobilized more rapidly, are ever seeking to rush the position, while reason, representing the desire and interest of the whole, strives to hold it until its slower mobilizing forces have time to gather and assert superiority.

The war has given new forms and contents to many of these struggles, and has sharpened their conscious intensity. Some of its consequences take shape in changed material conditions, others in attitudes of mind. The following stand among the "hardest" of the new facts with which the post-war world is called to reckon

1. The burdens of indebtedness, internal and external, which all the belligerent nations in different measures have to bear.

2. The alterations in the size and distribution of real incomes as between the different classes in the several nations, due to changes in prices, earnings and taxation brought about by war.
3. Changes in the respective wealth and income of different nations, their material resources, labour power, trade, shipping, credit.
4. Organization of capital in trusts and combinations, and of labour in trade unions, displacing competition by combination.
5. State regulation of supplies, prices, wages, profits.
6. The shift in the balance of sex-numbers, with its reactions upon marriage and the economic status of women.
7. The decline of the birth-rate, and the reduction of populations effected by war.
8. The concentration of the control over the larger part of the backward countries of the world in the hands of Great Britain and France.
9. The establishment of the forms of democratic government over a wider section of the world, by the overthrow of autocracies or oligarchies and the substitution of representative institutions upon the basis of adult suffrage. This makes a swift completion of the process by which the forms of political power have passed from the upper or the middle to the working classes.

These facts, stirring new feelings, are everywhere giving new shape to certain human problems of transcendent importance.

The race problem will assume a new complexity and intensity. The relation of the white races to the coloured races is vitally affected by (1) the enlistment and use of coloured troops in a white men's war; (2) the extension of Western control over an increasing portion of the coloured races in Africa and Asia, whether the control be national or international; (3) the conflicting political and economic policies announced for the treatment of colonies, protectorates or mandated areas, under the different White Powers, and the more rapid and organized exploitation of the tropics that will ensue.

The increased political and economic strength of Japan and her rapidly advancing career of imperialist exploitation in China give a new and a quickly growing prominence to the Yellow problem in the Pacific, perhaps with important reactions upon the structure and policy of the British Empire.

Failing the establishment of pacific internationalism upon a basis of substantial equality of opportunity for trade with tropical and other backward peoples, the political supremacy of two or three imperialist Great Powers will force a grouping of the other Powers in order to break this exclusive or preferential trade policy. The effective exclusion of Germany from equal access to oversea countries for trade and exploitation was an impelling cause of her war policy. The closer hold by a few Western Powers, and in particular by Britain, upon the greater part of the rich undeveloped resources of the world, must undoubtedly bring the excluded industrial nations into an armed alliance, with the object of challenging and breaking down an economic domination which directly injures their industrial development. The division of the Western world into imperial nations and non-imperial nations will give rise to a new dangerous system of competing alliances.

Within each nation the closer organization of capital and of labour, with new feelings of hostility, makes for a "class war," extending from industry to politics as these two spheres become more closely interlocked But within this general conflict arise by fission a number of special conflicts. Trades exposed to foreign competition, essential and key industries, infant industries, trusts and combinations, quasi-public industries, form special capitalistic interests which conflict with those of other trades in questions of tariffs, subsidies, taxation, price regulation and other governmental control. Within the ranks of labour similar conflicts exist, between strongly organized unions in essential industries, able to get high wages by forcing up prices, and the rest of the workers; between skilled and unskilled labour, overlapping industries, manual and brain workers, urban and rural, male and female. In addition to these sectional economic strifes, the class war in its general character is itself divided by the conflicting strategies of functional and local representation.

The sex conflict, gathering in the pre-war era, may take sharper and more disconcerting shapes, as the disturbance of the sex-balance compels larger numbers of women to invade the occupations hitherto reserved for men, and as the new consciousness of political and economic independence reacts upon the old conventions of male dominance in the family and the State.

I state these problems in terms of conflict, in order to given due emphasis to the greatest and most urgent of all our post-war issues. War has for five years enthroned force as the supreme arbiter in human affairs. Reason, justice, good will and compassion have been deposed from the rule of human conduct, and physical violence has been put in their place. Not merely the destinies of States and governments and the lives of armed men have been subjected to this rule, but the same force, divorced from justice or reason, has invaded every recess of private life in home or industry, brought pain, loss and misery to millions of innocent persons, annulled their liberties of speech and communications, movements, occupation and consumption. Nay, more than this, it has branded their minds and hearts with the belief that force was identical with right, and with the passionate desire that the force of their country should prevail.

This steeping of the collective and individual mind in force as the only way of settlement now forms the supreme danger in our confrontation of these post-war problems. The prolonged resort to force under the express sanction of every institution of organized prestige, Government, Church, Press, University and school, theatre, club, has left a general state of mind favourable to force as a panacea. The cowardly betrayal of reason and right by their authoritative guardians is the gravest of all the moral and intellectual damages of the war. For it has left a powerful predisposition to resort to force as the only practical settlement of each of the new problems. Class war is the direct fruit of this war-education. Right and reason are discredited, their moral and intellectual stock is low. Force with its mystical and emotional allies has invaded the provinces of religion and education. Our churches and schools are filled with the spirit of militant patriotism. The ritual of flag-worship which everywhere prevails is nothing but a thinly disguised appeal to force.

But against this rule of force, wielded by the separatist interests and passions for the pursuit of their special satisfactions, there stands the rule of reason wielded in the interests of humanity. Reason points to economic order, democracy and internationalism, to a pacific settlement of the conflicts we see sprouting from the battlefield. The salvation of the world lies in this assertion of the supremacy of reason. Can that supremacy be secured ? We know that peace sets in operation physical and other economic powers of recuperation astonishing in their strength and celerity. Is there not a corresponding tendency towards moral recuperation ? The extremity of the peril in which our world-order stands should rally those preservative instincts in man which make for the safety of the group. The new place of woman in the social counsels should be a double source of strength. For not only does woman represent more peculiarly the conservative race-preserving powers of nature, but she has been educated through the ages to gain her ends by methods of peaceful persuasion and moral strategy rather than by force.

But the mere existence of these preservative instincts and emotions does not suffice to safeguard our social order against the disintegrating forces that are at work. They must be mobilized in consciousness and furnished with effective means for making them prevail. An improved public opinion is the first essential for their operation. Thus education, in the wide sense of that word, emerges as the final issue. A free Press in the full meaning of that term, free not only from legal restraints but from economic bondage: free schools, not only in the sense that they are feeless and open to all willing students, but with no sectarian, social or political atmosphere or influence, open channels for the full flow of knowledge and its disinterested interpretation: churches and theatres which shall be vehicles for free thought and feeling in the service of humanity. Without these things an informed intelligent public opinion is impossible. To liberate, to cleanse and to improve these organs of opinions, so as to make them fit channels for the returning tide of reason, is the foremost task of all who are prepared to give themselves to the rescue of humanity from the material and moral wreckage of the war.

But the liberation of these channels for the free flow of socially creative energy cannot be achieved by any miraculous performance. The war has indeed stirred to their depths the social as well as the separatist passions of man. It has put new stores of faith, audacity and self-sacrifice at the service of mankind for the reconstruction of the world. In many countries the people have for the first time eaten of the tree of knowledge, and the bitter fruit has set their teeth on edge and upset their digestion. But the irritation thus generated will not supply the fund of revolutionary energy to which idealists and agitators often look to give explosive efficacy to their policies. Neither class-conscious idealism nor mass discontent, nor a combination of the two, can establish a new social order that will work, unless they co-operate with the technical transformation of the economic system which is taking place under the new scientific impulse.

Poverty will pull up sharply any other sort of revolution. Hope for the work cannot be found along the road of the new social idealism alone. The intensive and extensive application of the natural sciences, necessary to reduce the strain of toilsome industry upon the life of man and so release his powers of body and mind, his time and interest, for the free play of his personality and for non-economic intercourse, is an essential condition of a successful revolution. This is the true plea for productivity, the failure to respond to which will set a quite impenetrable barrier across the path of world recovery and progress. The crucial test for all post-war reconstruction is the plain economic question, "Does it increase productivity, thus liberating the worker from the burden of industrialism and enabling him to become a parent, an artist, a scholar and a human being."

INDEX

Printed in Great Britain by
UNWIN BROTHERS, LIMITED, THE GRESHAM PRESS, WOKING AND LONDON

For Product Safety Concerns and Information please contact our EU representative GPSR@taylorandfrancis.com
Taylor & Francis Verlag GmbH, Kaufingerstraße 24, 80331 München, Germany

www.ingramcontent.com/pod-product-compliance
Lightning Source LLC
LaVergne TN
LVHW021038011026
849160LV00008BA/431

* 9 7 8 0 4 1 5 8 2 3 2 4 1 *